Cybersecurity-Threat Hunting Process (C-THP) Roadmap—2ND EDITION

+ Mission Planning
+ Introduction to Cybersecurity Deception

Mark A. Russo, CISSP-ISSAP
Former Chief Information Security Officer, Department of Education

DEDICATION

This book is dedicated to my continually supportive instructors and professors at the National Defense University, Washington, DC, and their daily efforts to train and teach the next generation of cyber-warriors of this great Nation.

Cybersecurity-Threat Hunting Process (C-THP) Roadmap—2ND EDITION

by Mark A. Russo

Copyright © 2021 Cybersentinel, LLC. All rights reserved.

Printed in the United States of America.

2021: Jan – C version

Revision History for the
First Edition
Fourth version update:
March 13, 2021

Our Cybersecurity Blog Site

This is the major resource of everything, "Cyber."

"The good, the bad, and the ugly of cybersecurity all in one place."

Join us at https://cybersentinel.tech

This free resource is available to everyone interested in the fate and future of cybersecurity in the 21st Century

FREE FOR DOWNLOAD

Huawei Technologies: Chinese Risk to the International Supply Chain at
https://cybersentinel.tech/product/ebook-huawei-technologies-chinese-risk-to-the-international-supply-chain/

The Cybersecurity-Threat Hunting Process
2ND EDITION

This is a book for advanced cybersecurity personnel and demands additional resources to support its implementation.

In this SECOND EDITION, the author adds several key improvements. He adds a chapter on Mission Planning. How to create a tactical planning process from your Incident Response team to your Cybersecurity Threat Intelligence (CTI) analysts to your Hunt team? This version introduces readers to the growing interest and capabilities of Cyber-Deception as the next step in cyber-defense.

Table of Contents

PART I – The Strategic View **11**

The Big Picture 12

The Role of Cyber-Deception.. 18

The Importance of Incident Response (IR) 25

The Threat is China 29

PART II - An Introduction to the Process **35**

Cybersecurity-Threat Hunting Process.. 36

Threat Inputs 37

Hunting Activity 42

Conduct Review... 46

Characteristics of a Successful Hunt Mission 47

Event/Incident Outputs 48

C-THP Action Trees 49

Hunting Request (Externally focused)... 49

Base Hunting (Internally focused) 66

The Role of Metrics 75

Weekly Metrics... 75

Monthly Metrics.. 75

Annual Metrics 76

Qualitative versus Quantitative Metrics...76

PART III - Tactical Activities.................................83

C-THP Tactical Methodology 84

    84

Designate 86

Acquire 90

Analyze 94

Reporting 98

PART IV – Mission Planning 101

The Truly Tactical Portion of C-THP 102

C-THP Mission Planning..102

The "Optimal" THREAT Task Organization 103

PART V – Appendices...107

Appendix A – Relevant Terms and Glossary 108

Appendix B – Continuous Monitoring's Importance to the
C-THP 114

Appendix C -- Predictive Analytics: The Potential Role for
Process Improvement...128

Appendix D -- Can the Human "Poet" Bring Value to
Predictive Analysis?..137

Appendix E – The Threat Hunting Execution Order
Template 141

Appendix F – Threat Assessment Report (TAR) 146

Appendix G – The 10-Step Threat Hunting Mission Planning
Workflow...150

About the Author...153

LEGEND:

 A major change from version 1.

 Based in part or whole by contributions from readers of version 1.

 Special emphasis added by the author for the reader.

PART I – The Strategic View

The Cybersecurity Threat Hunting Process[1] (C-THP) is an ***active-passive defense activity*** coordinated between Incident Response (IR), the Threat Hunting, and the Cyber Threat Intelligence (CTI) teams. It is not OFFENSIVE and is used to assess whether an ***event is event-***based upon available and immediate intelligence. An event may or may not be raised to a defined ***incident***. The IR team is charged with determining whether the event should be presented to an actual incident for timely response activities acted upon by the Hunting Team in coordination with assigned CTI analysts.

Defensive Cybersecurity: The Relationship between Threat Hunting & CTI

The IR team may or may not always direct a **hunt** to be initiated until information from the CTI team reaches established thresholds for action. This is usually determined through established Standard Operating Procedures (SOP)

---

[1] The term "hunting" is used specifically for the personnel and processes that support the C-THP activities. The term "hunt" is used more broadly.

and organizational risk management policies. The IR team will evaluate the potential or actual level of risk posed by the intrusion.

OCCURRENCE → EVENT → INCIDENT
(less defined/initial) → (defined/confirmed/high impact)

The *Incident Response Spectrum* (below) describes the major activities that the IR team may implement—the offense or a "hack-back" is seldom authorized or recommended against any threat level[2]. The C-THP defines the IR team's actions, reviews by Cybersecurity Threat Intelligence (CTI), and coordinates operational Threat hunting personnel, for example, system administrators, coders, and forensics analysts, to attribute, deter, dissuade, deceive, or defeat malicious activities. C-THP is the first line of defense by internal experts to respond rapidly to threats to the Information Technology (IT) environment.

---

[2] A **Hack-back** is not recommended. Actions, especially against nation-state hackers, may result in far more damage by the hacker than initiating an attack against the threat target. The best course of action is determining the attribution of the attackers and reporting as part of an established Incident Response Plan (IRP) to authorities.

Incident Response Spectrum

-Assesses and reduces/stops malicious actors from within the network

-Determines level and kind of threat posed by a malicious actor [Cyber Threat Intelligence]-

Active	Offense
Passive	Defense

-Directly confronts or attacks malicious actors

-Creates an environment that prevents attacks or intrusions by a malicious actor

Both public agencies and private companies use the C-THP. ***This is a resource-intensive operation*** and typically is sought by medium and large companies needing to protect their critical data, information, Intellectual Property (IP), or government data from unauthorized access. The C-THP further defines how the hunting process functions and interacts with other features and processes. These procedures provide CTI Analysts, both within the CTI and within the Hunting teams, respectively, with methods to identify malicious cyber-activities throughout the operational IT environment.

Significant elements of C-THP are identified below. This provides a high-level overview of the complementary cybersecurity functions with a specific emphasis and focuses on the Hunting process.

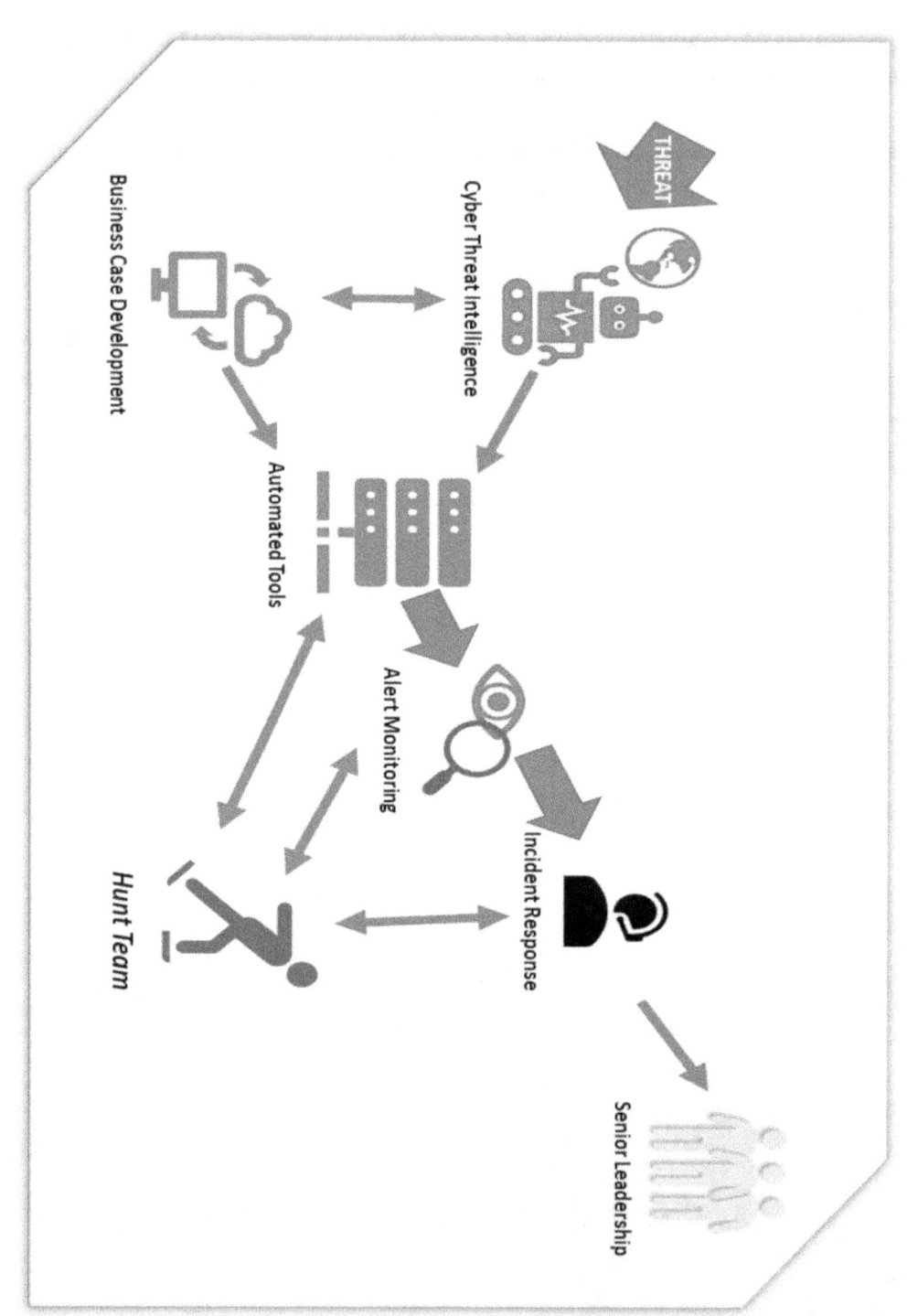

The process provides high-confidence, repeatability, and identification of cybersecurity events and incidents. ***Business Case Development (BCD)*** provides ***potential future scenarios*** and ***feedback*** to the C-THP to improve response personnel actions. BCD is designed to model and define capabilities to conduct follow-on responses and forensic activities. It receives inputs primarily[3] from the following four areas:

1. **Cyber Threat Intelligence (CTI)**

2. **Automated Tools**

3. **Business Case Development (BCD)**

4. **Incident Response (IR)**

Manual and automated continuous monitoring applications and devices are critical to C-THP success. Specifically, ***Continuous Monitoring*** (ConMon) is an integral component of the effective implementation of the National Institute for Standards and Technology's (NIST) Risk Management Framework (RMF). ConMon provides the next evolution in real progress within cybersecurity; it has yet to be achieved by most companies and agencies. See Appendix B, ***Continuous Monitoring's Importance to the C-THP***, for a more in-depth discussion of the role of ConMon and its direct support.

---

[3] Other inputs may include information from public alert websites/feeds and the federal government specific to their role or industry.

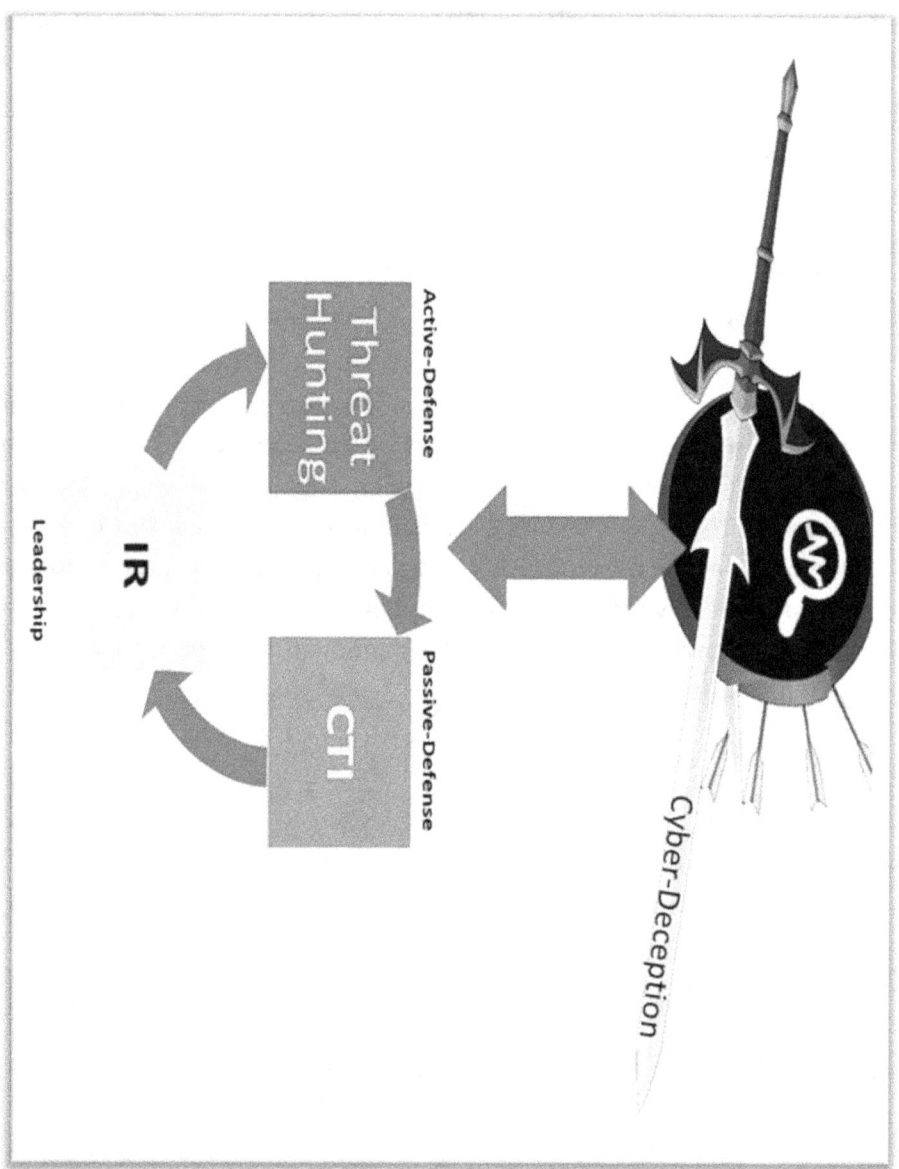

What do we do when our failed efforts have been focused for too long on Prevention alone?

Prevention has been less-than-successful for the defense of our modern-day networks. Daily we hear about another cyber-intrusion, and pure automated solutions such as deploying smart firewalls, anti-virus software, etc., have not stopped the "bad guys." An emerging and related capability that could enhance C-THP is the advent of Cybersecurity Deception (CD) as an adjunct to any reasonable C-THP effort. A move to a holistic CD planning and execution approach offers a serious solution to countering cyber-threat attackers' daily barrage. CD is the next opportunity for the Cybersecurity community to create a next-generation model for future success.

CYBER-DECEPTION (CD): Deliberate actions to obfuscate the threat from collecting complete and actionable intelligence about a defended Information Technology (IT) security boundary.

The classic solution for *deception* has been the honeypot in the realm of cybersecurity. *Norton* defines honeypots "...as a computer or computer system intended to mimic likely targets of cyberattacks. It can be used to detect attacks or deflect them from a legitimate target. It can also be <u>used to gain information about how cybercriminals operate</u>.[4]" It is not only about cybercriminals, but nation-state actors, individuals, and "hive minds" such as *Anonymous*; the honeypot, is just one typical example that offers both an active and passive form of cybersecurity defense.

CD employs three main elements for success which include:
1. Passive collection of intelligence to thwart future attacks (CTI)
2. Active measures to close vulnerabilities from within the network in coordination with an organization or company C-THP.
3. Holistic defense of the infrastructure through a coordinated effort

The nature of honeypot-like solutions is their existence and appearance as an actual targeted network. It is the purest form of cyber-deception. However, if it is not implemented in a convincing or reputable manner to the would-be attacker, it can be

---

[4] Norton. (2019). *What is a honeypot? [Blog post]. Retrieved from* *https://us.norton.com/internetsecurity-iot-what-is-a-honeypot.html*

easily dismissed and bypassed. The threat may recognize this as deception and further attempt to penetrate the actual network; ***the effort to establish a misleading environment is only as reasonable as its appearance as a genuine working IT environment.*** The more active-passive approach results from the simple IT deception in coordination with a more engaging collection of information/intelligence about an attacker and his Tactics, Techniques, and Procedures (TTP).

Passive

-Deception & Intelligence Collection

Active-Passive

-Mimics, Deceives, & Collects Intelligence

Active

-Mimics an IT Network

The Defensive Model for Cyber-Deception

What more is needed?

It is vital to implement a ***Strategic Cybersecurity Deception Plan (SCDP)*** within the deception lifecycle. It should be composed of the following elements:

1. GOALS/OBJECTIVES: What can you accomplish within your available resources? Can you develop multiple virtualized database servers with dummy data or employ a single server behind the firewall that creates a diversion from your primary data repositories? Two major sub-components should constrain your goals and objectives:

    a. Resources: People, dollars, and skills, AND
    b. Risk tolerance: What damage may result in your company or agency based upon a data breach? Can your reputation survive a data loss, or are other mitigation strategies possible?

2. TACTICAL DECEPTION: How can you create a plausible IT environment that either causes the threat to be diverted from your infrastructure as a target or causes them to move elsewhere? Can you appear as a more complex environment that creates multiple false targets for an attacker?

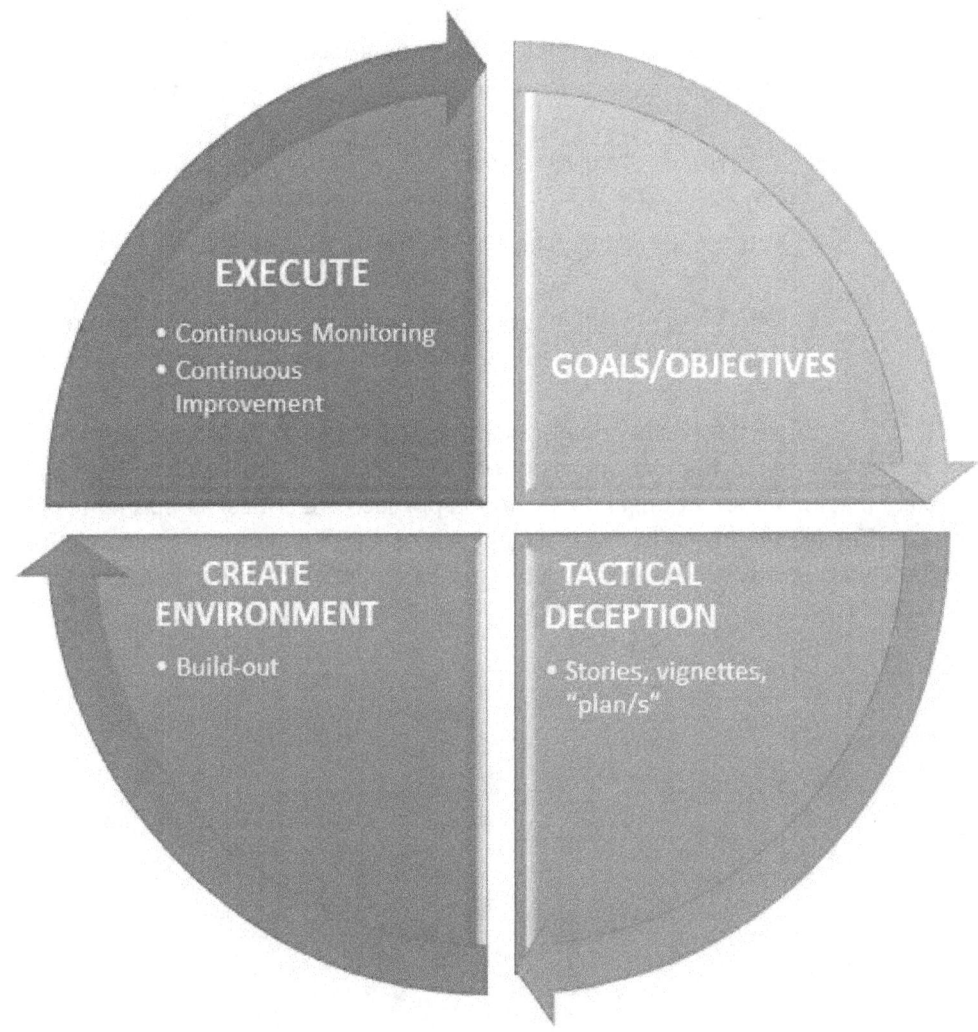

Strategic Cybersecurity Deception Plan (SCDP) Lifecycle

3. CREATE THE ENVIRONMENT: Apply the resources and deception plan into a physical environment. Identify what additional resources may be needed, such as specialized equipment or third-party security providers.

4. EXECUTE: At this point in the lifecycle, begin to conduct both passive and active operations to accomplish your primary goals/objectives. Additionally, this approach requires an ongoing review to include:

   a. CONTINUOUS MONITORING: Collect necessary threat data, such as Indicators of Compromise (IOC), such as file names, Internet Protocol (IP) addresses, hash "fingerprint" values, etc.

   b. CONTINUOUS IMPROVEMENT: Continue to appear as a legitimate network by adding and modifying the deception network over time.

   While this has been only an introduction to CD's concept, pure prevention from cyber-attack has not been successful. Cybersecurity Deception planning, implementation, and execution approach are critical components of any effective cybersecurity defensive measures. CD may be the next chance for the Cybersecurity community to deter, dissuade, and defeat the "bad guys."

The Importance of Incident Response (IR)

Incident Response (IR) <u>requires</u> a plan to include who or what agency is notified when a breach has occurred.

The main effort should be identifying with government representatives what constitutes a reportable event or, more importantly, an **incident**. This could include, for example, an actual breach that has occurred to the IT infrastructure by identified threats identified by Security Operation Center (SOC). Incidents could include anything from a Denial of Service (DOS) attack—overloading of outwardly facing web or mail servers-- or exfiltration of data—where Controlled Unclassified Information (CUI) data has been copied or moved to outside of the organization's firewall/perimeter. Incidents could also include the destruction of data that, for example, is identified through continuous monitoring and routine audit activities.

Secondarily, who do you notify? Do you alert, for example, an assigned Contract Officer Representative (COR), the Contract Office itself, Department of Defense's (DOD) US Cybercommand at Fort Meade, MD, or possibly the Department of Homeland Security's (DHS) Computer Emergency Response Team (CERT) (https://www.us-cert.gov/forms/report)? Cybersecurity personnel and senior leaders will have to determine where and file standard "incident" reports. External Reporting organizations should provide templates and forms specific to the agency's own unique reporting requirements. (See the paragraph below on DOD Precedence Categorization as a guide.)

Furthermore, IR requires the testing of the IR Plan (IRP) at least ***annually***. However, it is suggested that an organization's test more often. Until comfortable with the IR response plan and associated "reporting chain," ***practice, practice, practice***.

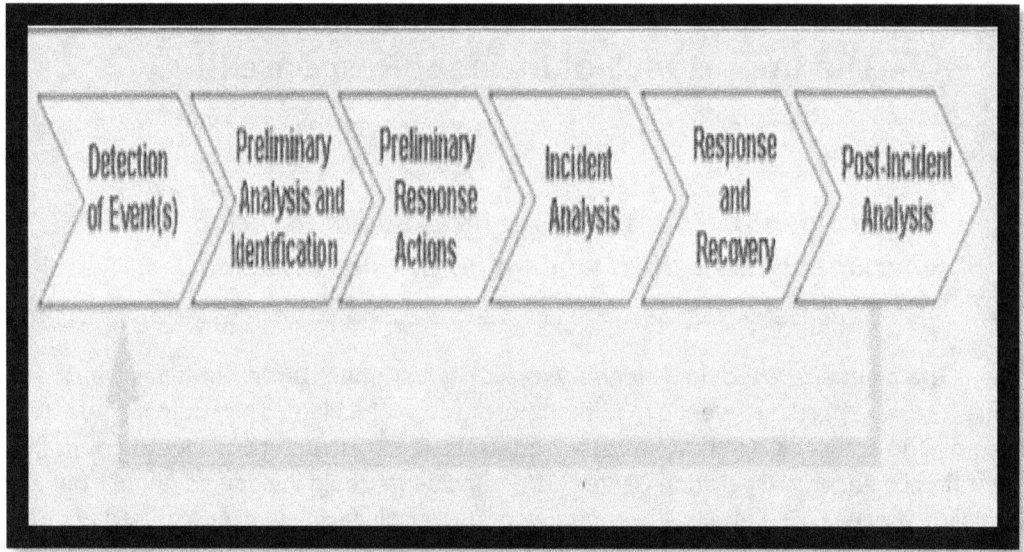

The DOD Cyber Incident Life Cycle. This diagram from the DOD is a representative example of a typical "incident response life cycle." It is intended to assist in IR activities and better assist in coordination with government cybersecurity incident response organizations. Recognizing this as either an "event" (not necessarily a negative occurrence) versus an "incident" is an internal determination by the leadership in coordination with its cybersecurity and IT professional staff to include the hunt team. An incident specifically requires alerting the government as soon as the intrusion is *recognized*.

Verify with the respective agency its reporting standards. Typically, **events** may not need to be reported based on the widespread impacts and workloads, especially government cybersecurity response organizations. In the case of **incidents**, the standard is 72-hours to submit a report; however, the recommendation is *as soon as possible* due to the potential impacts beyond the IT infrastructure. Furthermore, it can pose a serious direct threat to interconnected federal agency IT environments.

The chart below categorizes the current Department of Defense (DOD) and the Department of Homeland Security (DHS) common precedence designations. It provides both a standard categorization for identified events, and typically, precedence is used to determine the level of action and response depending on the priority "severity."

Precedence	Category	Description
0	0	Training and Exercises
1	1	Root Level Intrusion (Incident)
2	2	User Level Intrusion (Incident)
3	4	Denial of Service (Incident)
4	7	Malicious Logic (Incident)
5	3	Unsuccessful Activity Attempt (Event)
6	5	Non-Compliance Activity (Event)
7	6	Reconnaissance (Event)
8	8	Investigating (Event)
9	9	Explained Anomaly (Event)

DOD Precedence Categorization. Nine (9) is the lowest event where little is known, and IT personnel are attempting to determine whether this activity should be elevated to alert leadership or to "close it out." One (1) is a deep-attack. It identifies that the incident has gained "root" access. Root access can be construed as the intruder has complete access to the most restrictive security levels of a system. This type of access usually is interpreted to be complete and unfettered access to networks and data. (SOURCE: Cyber Incident Handling Program, CJCSM 6510.01B, 18 December 2014, http://www.jcs.mil/Portals/36/Documents/Library/Manuals/m651001.pdf?ver=2016-02-05-175710-897)

The Threat is China

No discussion of C-THP would be complete without discussing the major nation-state actors that pose a daily threat to the global community. While Russia, Iran, and North Korea or known active attackers, China represents the main threat for the foreseeable future. China considers using an "assassin's mace" the key to its worldwide dominance. Its application rests with its growing capabilities in cyberspace.

The Chinese see cybersecurity exploitation as a critical element of its asymmetric "warfare" against the West. The book, *The Hundred-Year Marathon* by Michael Pillsbury, provides a more extensive understanding of China's long-game strategy.

In February 2015, the Director of National Intelligence (DNI) identified one of the significant risks facing the United States (US) within the "Cyber" domain is the insertion of malicious code into Information Technology (IT) hardware and software items sold to the US. According to the DNI: "Despite ever-improving network defenses, the diverse possibilities for…supply chain operations to insert compromised hardware or software…will hold nearly all [Information and Communication Technology] systems at risk for years to come" (DNI, 2015, p.1).

While several foreign IT equipment and software companies have been accused of such activities, the major threat in this arena is the Chinese company _Huawei (Wah-way) Technologies Company, Limited_. In 2012, the House Permanent Select Committee on Intelligence had significant concerns. Specific to its investigation of the operating practices of Huawei, the committee reported that: "The threat posed [by Huawei/China] to U.S. national-security interests… in the telecommunications supply chain is an increasing priority…" (US House of Representatives, 2012, p.1).

While there are no specific unclassified details of such injections of malicious code into Huawei products, in 2006, a discreet ban by several Western nations, including the US, was initiated against the Chinese firm of **Lenovo** Personal Computers. Shortly after Lenovo purchased International Business Machine's (IBM) personal computing division, the use or purchase of Lenovo PCs "…due to backdoor vulnerabilities" (Infosec Institute, 2013) was banned.

Huawei represents a similar and more pervasive threat to the international IT supply chain. Huawei has both the means and motives to compromise IT equipment and systems on behalf of the Chinese government. "…Huawei has refused to explain its relationship with the Chinese government or the role of the Communist Party...inside the company..." (Simonite, 2012), and it can be assumed, based on multiple Huawei senior leaders with close ties with the People's Liberation Army (PLA), that Huawei has an explicit connection with the Chinese government.

As a surrogate for the Chinese government, the primary motivation for Huawei is to support its 5-year Plan focused on it becoming a dominant global economic super-power. Huawei is implicitly aligned with this plan that "State-owned enterprises are instructed to acquire assets perceived as valuable by Beijing" (Scissors, 2013). It continues a wide range of acquisitions to include mergers with American and other Western IT companies.

The PLA's Unit 61398 has been extensively analyzed by government and private cybersecurity firms. In 2013, **Mandiant** released an exhaustive and authoritative report based upon an in-depth analysis of code and techniques specific to Unit 61398. The most conclusive statement made was that the "...Communist Party of China is tasking the Chinese People's Liberation Army [Unit 61398 and others] to commit systematic cyber espionage and data theft..." (Mandiant, 2013, p. 7). It can be further agreed that some of that training, equipment, and expertise is provided by Huawei directly to the PLA. The **Far Eastern Economic Review** reported, "...Huawei received a key contract to supply the PLA's first national telecommunications network" (Ahrens, 2013). These ties point to connections with the Chinese government and the PLA; there is little doubt that China continues aggressive cyber-activities to support its intentions to increase its economic standing in the world.

China has not demonstrated a desire to defeat cyber-espionage activities from within its borders. It can be surmised that many Chinese cyber-activities are supported and controlled under the Chinese government's auspices. The most lucrative target for China, and more specifically Huawei, is the US; it will continue to focus its vast resources against US economic and business entities.

Additionally, Huawei has multiple cyber-relevant capabilities to include hardware and software development, IT manufacturing, and in-house technical expertise. However, the primary ability afforded Huawei is through its direct backing by the Chinese government. As noted, in terms of government contracts and resources, Huawei has powerful direct support.

In terms of its infrastructure, it is vast and vibrant. Access to the Internet as a hidden mechanism to hide its activities is another potential threat posed by Huawei to subvert the world's IT architecture. By leveraging its internal infrastructure, it has near limitless capabilities to disrupt the US and its allies via the Internet in conjunction with the Chinese state.

According to Lachow, Huawei as a sophisticated agent, would require "...a team of individuals (or perhaps multiple teams) with expertise in several technical areas..." (Lachow, 2008, p. 444). Huawei, in coordination with the PLA (or vice versa), has access to formidable resources. The PLA is reaching out across a wide swath of [the] Chinese civilian sector to meet the intensive requirements necessary to support its burgeoning [Information Warfare] capabilities, incorporating people with specialized skills from commercial industry..." (Krekel, 2009, p. 7).

Huawei should be expected to use the Internet for passive cyber-espionage collection activities mostly; however, it can engage in more active operations. This could include establishing secretive Command and Control (C2) nodes within its own sold equipment and software and in "infected" competitors' equipment sold in the international marketplace. With this access, it could pose a formidable offensive capability.

Huawei has a considerable target-set to pursue. With its growth throughout the global IT marketplace, any nation requiring IT products offers a target-rich environment for Huawei to exploit. Targets available to Huawei are wide-ranging and span the entire developed and industrial countries that conduct regular business with Huawei.

All countries are potentially exploitable, especially in terms of their reliance on the Internet. The need for computer hardware and software by all developed nations affords a consistent and regular vulnerability. It can be surmised that Huawei personnel have the requisite knowledge and ability to exploit all levels of its manufactured products (and those of its competitors); this capability provides a direct ability to align with Beijing's motivations, the predominant economic powerhouse of the world.

In terms of cyber-espionage, the magnitude is more significant than $445 B annually "...to the world economy" (Nakashima & Peterson, 2014) as identified in a 2014 *Washington Post* article. If the allegations against Huawei are correct, the potential economic loss to the world could be far more significant if Huawei has expanded the capacity to process the volumes of exfiltrated data. The graver implications would be damage to the global economy, more in the trillions of dollars annually in stolen intellectual property and data.

The severest and the more exploitive consequence would be Huawei could have the ability to leverage injected malicious code in its products. This would imply the ability to shutdown portions of the entire Internet because of its control of foundational backbones hardware devices such as routers, switches, and firewalls. While the ongoing cyber-espionage economic losses to countries are severe, it can inflict massive offensive harm against governments or groups that in the future it may be in conflict to include the US.

Conclusion

Huawei is a **sophisticated** threat. Lachow reserves this label to highly coordinated and effective state actors with nearly unlimited resources. Huawei is such a threat with the essential skillsets to a very diverse and technologically capable adversary. With the Chinese government's presumptive backing and its resources, Huawei continues to be a significant threat to US and international governments and their respective economies.

While there is no conclusive or public evidence that China, through its surrogate Huawei, has injected malicious coding into any of its products, the risk is formidable. Michael Maloof, a former senior security policy analyst in the Office of the Secretary of Defense, ascribe from sources that "[t]he Chinese government reportedly has "pervasive access" to some 80 percent of the world's communications, thanks to backdoors it has ordered to be installed in devices made by Huawei" (Protalinski, 2012). Jim Lewis, at the Center for Strategic and International Studies, provides an ominous point of view working with Chinese businesses: "The Chinese will tell you that stealing technology and business secrets [are] a way of building their economy and that this is important for national security" (Metz, 2013). The Chinese regime directly threatens the risk to the US's national security, its economic viability, and its critical infrastructure.

References for "The Threat is China"

Ahrens, N. (2013, February). *China's Competitiveness: Myth, Reality and Lessons for the United States and Japan*. Retrieved from Center for Strategic and International Studies: http://csis.org/files/publication/130215_competitiveness_Huawei_casestudy_Web.pdf

Barbozaaug, D. (2010, August 22). *Scrutiny for Chinese Telecom Bid*. Retrieved from New York Times: http://www.nytimes.com/2010/08/23/business/global/23telecom.html?_r=0

DNI. (2015, February 26). *Statement of Record: Worldwide Threat Assessment*. Retrieved from http://www.armed-services.senate.gov/imo/media/doc/Stewart_02-26-15.pdf

Infosec Institute. (2013, October 11). *Hardware attacks, backdoors and electronic component qualification*. Retrieved from Infosec Institute: http://resources.infosecinstitute.com/hardware-attacks-backdoors-and-electronic-component-qualification/

Krekel, B. (2009, October 9). *Capability of the People's Republic of China to Conduct Cyber Warfare and Computer Network Exploitation*. Retrieved from George Washington University: http://nsarchive.gwu.edu/NSAEBB/NSAEBB424/docs/Cyber-030.pdf

Lachow, I. (2008). Cyber Terrorism: Menace or Myth. *Cyber Power*, 19-20.

Mandiant. (2013, February 18). *APT1: Exposing One of China's Cyber Espionage Units*. Retrieved from Mandiant: http://intelreport.mandiant.com/Mandiant_APT1_Report.pdf

Metz, C. (2013, December 31). *U.S. to China: We Hacked Your Internet Gear We Told You Not to Hack*. Retrieved from Wired: http://www.wired.com/2013/12/nsa-cisco-huawei-china/

Nakashima, E., & Peterson, A. (2014, June 9). *Report: Cybercrime and espionage costs $445 billion annually*. Retrieved from Washington Post: http://www.washingtonpost.com/world/national-security/report-cybercrime-and-espionage-costs-445-billion-annually/2014/06/08/8995291c-ecce-11e3-9f5c-9075d5508f0a_story.html

Protalinski, E. (2012, July 14). *Former Pentagon analyst: China has backdoors to 80% of telecoms*. Retrieved from ZDNet: http://www.zdnet.com/article/former-pentagon-analyst-china-has-backdoors-to-80-of-telecoms/

Scissors, D. P. (2013, May 9). *Chinese Investment in the U.S.: Facts and Motives*. Retrieved from Heritage Society: http://www.heritage.org/research/testimony/2013/05/chinese-investment-in-the-us-facts-and-motives

Simonite, T. (2012, October 9). *Why the United States Is So Afraid of Huawei*. Retrieved from
MIT Technology Review: http://www.technologyreview.com/news/429542/why-the-
united-states-is-so-afraid-of-huawei/

US House of Representatives. (2012, October 8). *Investigative Report on the US National
Security Issues Posed by Chinese Telecommunications Companies Huawei and ZTE*.
Retrieved from
https://intelligence.house.gov/sites/intelligence.house.gov/files/documents/Huawei-
ZTE%20Investigative%20Report%20(FINAL).pdf

PART II - An Introduction to the Process

Cybersecurity-Threat Hunting Process

   "Hunting" follows the process outlined below. This ensures that all Hunting provides feedback and value to the company, business, or agency. It requires a consistent and repeatable response. The C-THP also requires a "continual improvement" element like many mainstream development processes such as, for example, the Information Technology Information Library® (ITIL). Continual improvement requires after-action meetings, training, and outside third-party evaluation on a recurring basis. These are measures designed to improve the organizations' cybersecurity threat response activities and capabilities.

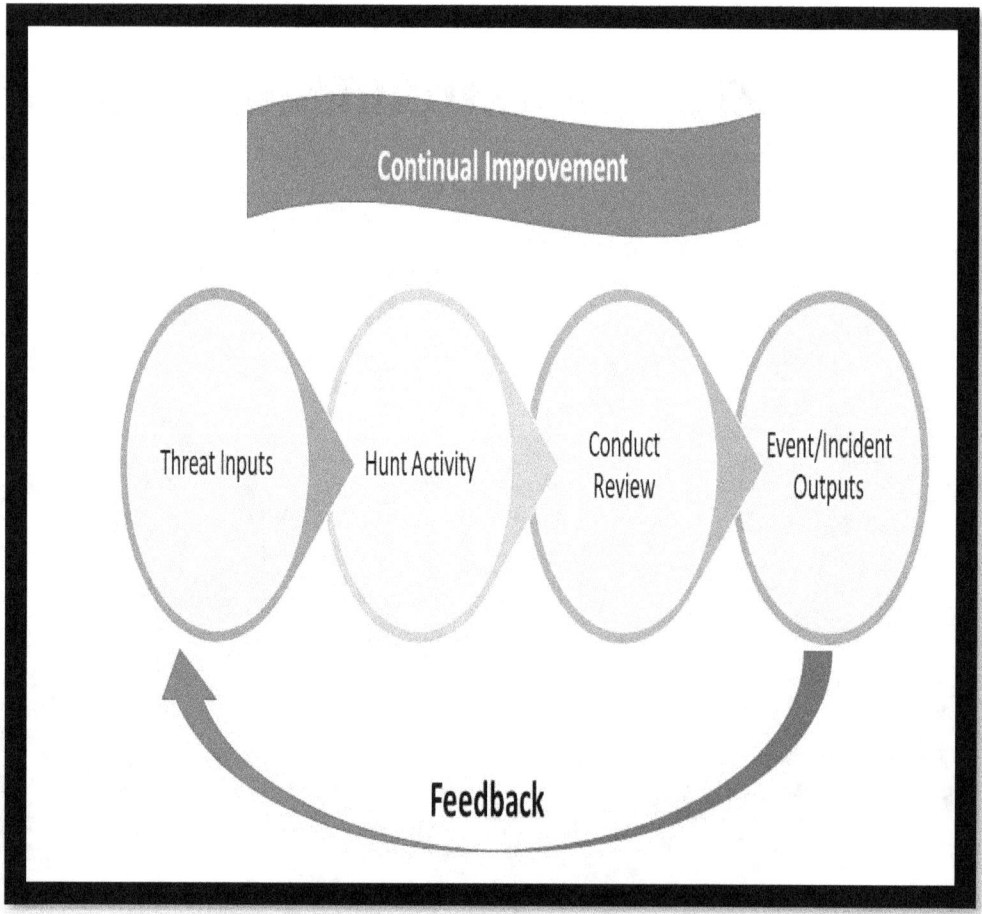

Threat Inputs

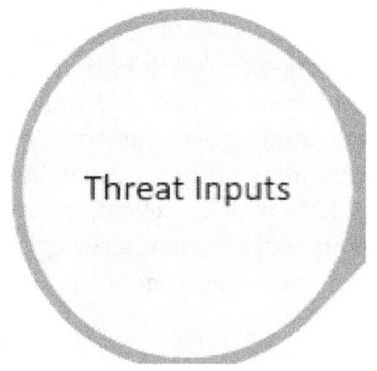

Threat Inputs

CTI Analysts directly support the Hunting process. They are involved in both the first passive collection of information or intelligence that anticipates or detects an attack into the IT environment and as main contributors for reports, products, and analysis designed to support leadership goals and objectives. CTI analysts are responsible for the management of the Intelligence Cycle.

The Intelligence Cycle is the overall collection process of the Intelligence cycle. The **Intelligence Cycle** is the fundamental approach used by the US and international intelligence agencies. It is used by civilians, military **intelligence**, or law enforcement agencies. "The stages of the intelligence cycle include the issuance of requirements by decision-makers, collection, processing, analysis, and publication of intelligence. The circuit is completed when decision-makers provide feedback and revised requirements. The intelligence cycle is an effective way of processing information and turning it into relevant and actionable intelligence".[5]

The Intelligence Process

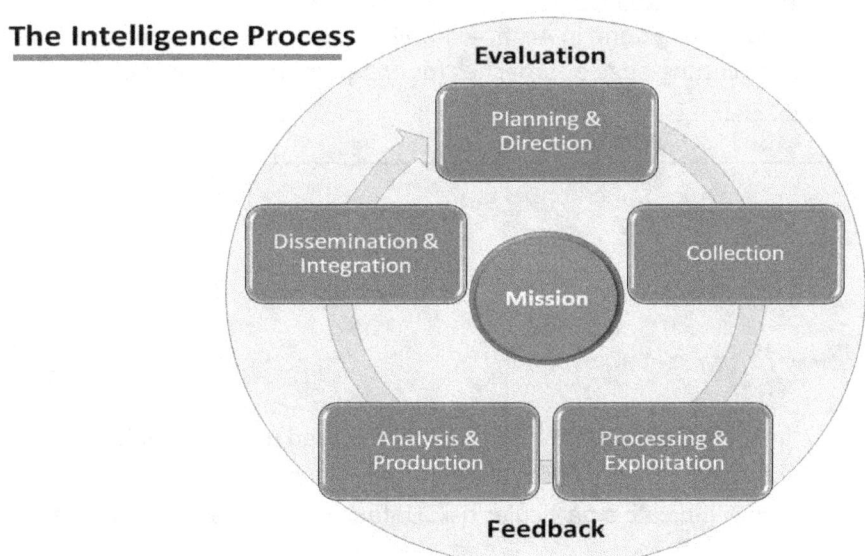

Source: Joint Intelligence/Joint Publication 2-0 (Joint Chiefs of Staff)

---

[5] https://en.wikipedia.org/wiki/Intelligence_cycle

Hunting requests[6] or **base hunts** are initiated by leadership and, more typically, by the Incident Response Team. Both manual and automated processes manage the action, but all history and data are captured in a developed **Master Threat Hunting Database (MTHDB).** The MTHDB is a defined repository that tracks Indicators of Compromise (IOC) that assist in determining who and what level of attack is deployed based upon such indicators, intelligence, patterns of attack, etc., that helps in formulating a better understanding of threat capabilities and motivations within the targeted IT environment. IOCs may be developed from internal experts, but there are several low-cost, and no-cost solutions already deployed for the public and private sectors use for companies and agencies. These include, for example, are:

1. FireEye's ® publicly shared IOC's of Github at https://github.com/fireeye/iocs
2. The DHS shares Joint Indicator Bulletins at https://www.us-cert.gov/ncas/bulletins
3. DHS also offers Automated Indicator Sharing (AIS). More information on how to integrate with these services may be found at https://www.dhs.gov/ais
4. Crowdstrike® also offers IOC access via its Falcon Query API. More information can be found at https://www.crowdstrike.com/blog/tech-center/import-iocs-crowdstrike-falcon-host-platform-via-api/
5. Also, work being done in Artificial Intelligence (AI) by the company Cylance® provides cutting-edge approaches for end-point protection. See www.cylance.com

 Classic versus Next-Generation IOC

Classic Indicators of Compromise (C-IOC) are based upon heuristic, static, "rules of thumb." If a threat commonly uses a specific malicious file, for example, *malware.exe*, it may indicate a particular risk. Unfortunately, the threats, especially the

---

[6] **Hunt** requests are typically triggered by outside detected events and **base hunts** are used to assess organizational and individual compliance with Acceptable Use Policies (AUP) covering organizational personnel.

nation-state actors, typically obfuscate their true identities in cyberspace and change their digital signature.

A typical example is where threats add additional code to change their original file's hash value. In the example, malware.exe, adding two to three other code lines (or just meaningless ## comment lines), changes the file size by several kilobytes. The result is the original digital fingerprint, even though it is the same malicious code, no longer has the defined IOC digital hash value. It has changed, but the malicious file has not.

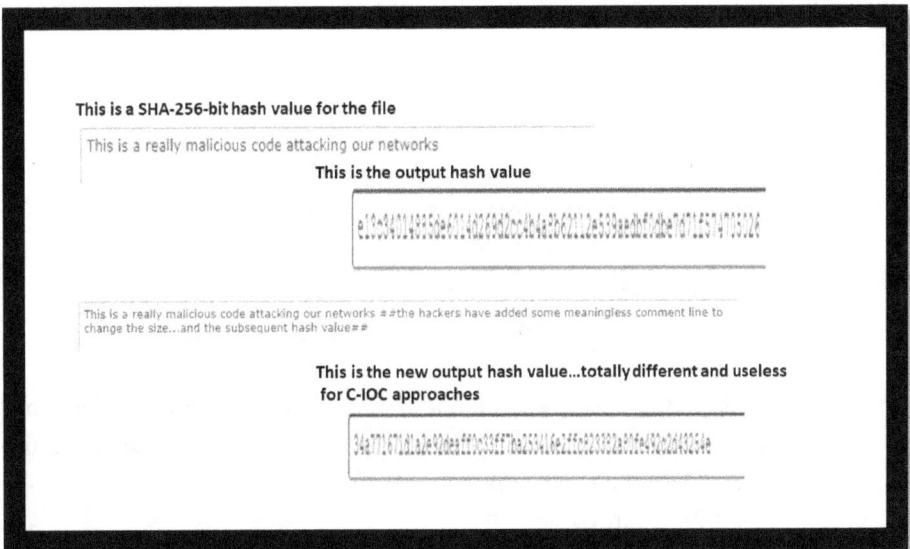

Other changes causing C-IOCs to be less-effective include the threat of employing, for example, "spoofing" of their Internet Protocol (IP) addresses, using "The Onion Router"[7] (TOR) to hide their identity. TOR uses proxy servers across the globe to mask actual IP addresses and attribution.

Additional issues with C-IOC are that they are vulnerable (and useless) against zero-day exploits that they hold in reserve to attack high-priority targets. The C-IOC provides a start but has been proving for years to be value-less in identifying actual threats and confirmation of their attribution.

C-IOC can be categorized by **Means, Motives, and Opportunities (MMO).** Law enforcement and the intelligence community have attempted, with the private sector's aid, to categorize and defend against cyber-threats. The following are examples of how C-IOC may be used:

---

[7] See https://en.wikipedia.org/wiki/Tor_(anonymity_network)

- **Identify Means (technical).** This will include digital and technological signatures to isolate the culprit, organization, or nation.
    - Malicious software hash values
    - Embedded language (natural and programming)
    - Biometric (keystroke, behavioral, etc.)

- **Identify Motivations.** What is driving the hacker to attack your network or IT environment?
    - Financial
    - Data
        - Access
        - Exfiltration
        - Destruction
        - Modification/Manipulation
    - Establishing a "foothold" for future operations
    - Denial of Services (DOS)
    - Elevate privileges to access targeted data
    - Attack reputation of the target

- **Identify Opportunities.** The ideal opportunity is through poor cyber-hygiene to include not patching systems and network infrastructures.
    - Network vulnerabilities
    - Zero-day exploits
    - Physical vulnerabilities ("social engineering")

What will better describe the next evolution of IOC? The Next Generation IOC (NG-IOC) will likely occur due to the growth within the various data science fields; these include artificial intelligence, machine learning, Artificial Neural Networks, Big Data, etc. The more extraordinary collection and processing capabilities of Big Data, for example, will create a more capable and responsive ability to detect and respond to threats. Threats will not be able to obfuscate and avoid identification with such expanded measures altogether.

NG-IOC will be able to "deconstruct" the threat's means. The NG-IOC will better analyze patterns quickly and access law enforcement and other databases to correlate and attribute the threat. It will further include advancements in identifying threat motivations, and it will connect entities that have in the past conducted acts against like targets. It will consist of predictive analytics to anticipate specific entities likely to be the actual threat. NG-IOC will also identify past weaknesses and poor cyber-hygiene practices on the part of a company or agency and notify them how to respond accordingly.

However, the natural synergy will occur based upon data science's holistic application using machine learning and Artificial Neural Network (ANN) to analyze MMO collectively. Data science promises to glean specific, actionable insights far faster than any team of CTI analysts.

NG-IOC will ultimately provide critical strengths: the ability to provide real-time and predictive analysis of the Threat Hunting team threat. (Also, see the following Appendices covering data science and predictive analysis in support of cybersecurity and threat hunting: Appendix C, *"Predictive Analytics: The Potential Role for Process Improvement,"* and Appendix D, *"Can the Human "Poet" Bring Value to Predictive Analysis?"*)

Big Data Emergence

The emergence of the term cyber analytics has entered the realm of cybersecurity protection considerations. It is a union between cybersecurity challenges and leveraging data science to address better relentless cyber-attacks (Djekic, 2019; National Association of State Chief Information Officers [NASCIO] 2016). There are many existing statistical and ever-growing data modeling-predictive capabilities arising from the field of data science (Loy, 2019; Silver, 2012). Specifically, the growth of data science is, in part, attributable to the availability and increase of Big Data repositories and other supportive and underlying technologies (Taylor-Sakyi, 2016).

Big data is providing a critical foundation of much of the current capabilities of Artificial Intelligence (AI) and Machine Learning (ML) tools and solutions (Fang, Xu, M., Xu, S., & Zhao, 2019; Wilner, 2018; Yu-Zhong, Zi-Gang, Xu, & Ying-Cheng, 2015). AI mechanisms, such as the Artificial Neural Network (ANN), aid in better decision-making and offer significant improvements in countering cyber-threats (Chimento, 2019; Fang et al., 2019; Gupta & Rani, 2018; Halladay, 2013; K & Shivakumar, 2014).

Current capabilities of ML Predictive Analytics (PA) and the availability of massive amounts of Big Data datasets provide the potential for greater depth for companies or agencies "to lower...costs...and improve overall efficiencies" (Nagrecha & Chawla, 2016, p. 1). Companies are embracing data science methods to "not only deliver value from their internal data but also to connect with external data sources to develop a complete data profile [of the threat]" (p. 1). The merger of the problems of detecting and protecting organizational networks with data science capabilities offers the next evolution in the battle against threats in cyberspace.

Hunting Activity

Hunting requests may originate from the following three functional areas: CTI, BCD, or IR. Any final determination for the action is the IR team's responsibility and will be based upon risk and immediacy in protecting the IT environment. It will be in coordination with senior leadership/management for action, alert, and visibility purposes

1. **Cyber Threat Intelligence (CTI)** – Internally/externally sourced CTI, including operational Communities of Interest (CoI), Government Partners, Law Enforcement, etc. Based upon the CTI review of the available intelligence, it may "tip" a potential Hunting activity to IR for action.

2. **Business Case Development** – Feedback on a **rule creation**[8] request is received by the business case development process/team. The BCD determines whether a hunt is needed based upon changes in the IT environment. These may include:

   a) When a hunt should be performed due to known or anticipated changes in TTPs by threat entities [proactive], and new business cases, or,

   b) When it would not be feasible to create an automated rule for the request. A manual hunt is necessary due to the threat of TTP changes. It is essential to refine the business case of the identified threat. *Is more information needed to provide a fuller picture of the threat?*

3. **Incident Response** – Indicators of Compromise supplied by the CTI or like external organizations have identified a potential threat vector or actual attack. IR will direct Hunting resources as appropriate to initiate a hunt. *This is the primary source and de facto leader over the C-THP.*

---

[8] **Rule creation** can be either applied in a manual manner by a CTI analyst or more likely as a "rule" implemented within automated security devices to include firewalls, Intrusion Prevention Systems (IPS), or Security Information Event Management (SIEM) devices.

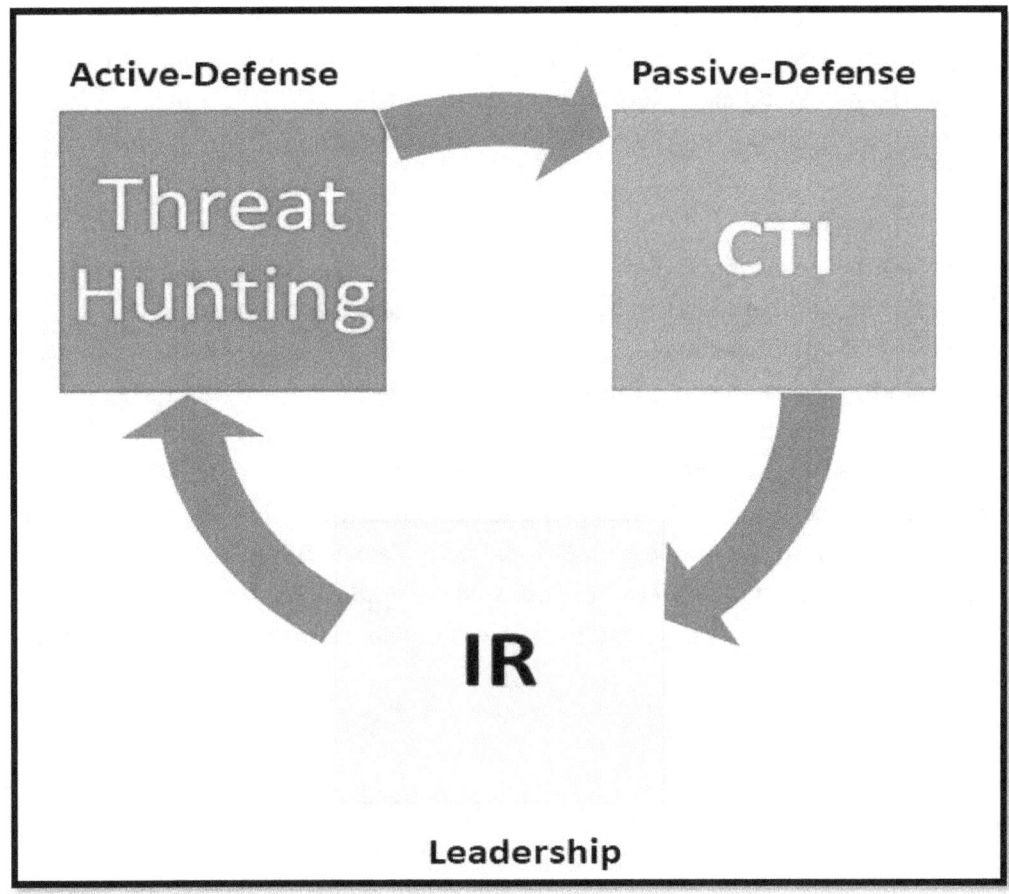

Incident Response Leads the C-THP

Hunting

Hunting is ***typically*** focused against external attackers but may also include "insider threat" activities. Using inputs, a CTI may also initiate, in coordination with IR, a C-THP activity/hunt upon direction and authorization. Hunting consists of selecting the proper tools, collecting data from existing tools/data sources, analyzing the results, and documenting outcomes. CTI analysts perform an iterative process by querying the tools, reviewing the data, filtering out known or non-malicious behavior, and re-querying the data. This continues until malicious activities are found and identified.[9] Analysts will either use existing tools, create, or procure new means to fulfill the hunt's needs.

---

[9] "Identified" relates to known IOC signatures, but does not ignore deception or spoofing by the cyber-threat.

Gaps in tool capabilities should be documented and reviewed by corporate or agency leadership. This may include Senior IR Personnel or specialized experts to have the assigned Chief Information Security Officer (CISO). This includes funding and resourcing priorities and effective processes.

Base Hunting

Base Hunting is typically internally focused on ***matters of compliance.*** It is defined as repeatable searches based on an analytical methodology that produces low-fidelity results (i.e., results that require analyst review and cannot be fully automated as a rule). These Hunts will reside in the MTHDB. Base Hunting, for example, may leverage tools such as FireEye HX® technology; this technology obtains endpoint intelligence that may include but is not limited to Windows Services listing, Windows Scheduled Task listing, Windows Registry Run keys, and the Windows Application Compatibility Cache. ***Tools should assist in any determination of whether alterations or manipulations of critical services have occurred.*** This may also lead to follow-on review and correction by trained personnel.

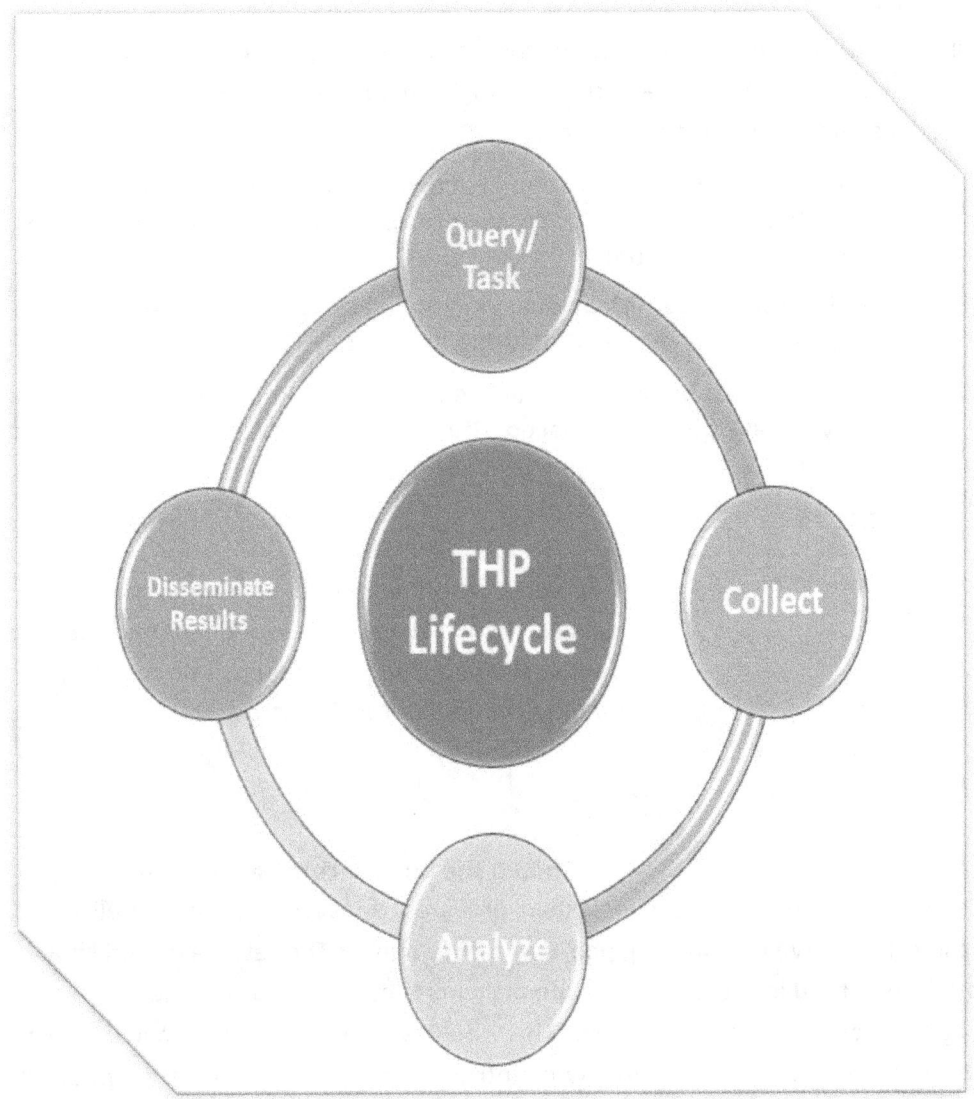

The C-THP Lifecycle

Upon completion of a review of the data, analysts will document the outcomes of their findings.

Outcomes

All hunts *will end in one of three outcomes*. Based on Hunting's product, an analyst will document the results accordingly and distribute them to other functions and processes as necessary.

1. **Nothing Discovered.** No indication of active compromise or behavior violating identified best practices, acceptable use, or organizational policies discovered during the hunt.

2. **Something Found: Non-Malicious.** Violation(s) of acceptable use or organizational policy discovered during the hunt.

3. **Something Found: Malicious.** An active or historic compromise, which may currently or have previously placed, IT assets or its data at risk, is discovered.

Conduct Review

To ensure that the hunt team's analysts remain focused on relevant and essential hunts, analysts must evaluate completed hunts and move all hunts possible to the BCD process.

Should the hunt become a base hunt?

Does the analyst believe the logic used provides repeatable and low-fidelity results that serve as a starting point for future hunts? The rationale used should be documented in the MTHDB. Is the malicious actor from within the organization or has unique access? This would warrant initiating a follow-on Base Hunting action for potential follow-on intrusions requiring continual monitoring.

Can the hunt become a rule?

If an analyst determines that a hunt may become a business rule, Hunt's documentation should be delivered to the business case development process. The information should be formulated into a rule applied to monitoring and alert devices[10] on the network; this, too, should be transferred to the MTHDB. The

---

[10] "Smart" network devices may include firewalls, Intrusion Detection/Prevention Systems, or Security Incident Event Monitoring (SIEM) hardware.

hunt team is responsible for documenting the methodology followed within the MTHDB and providing this information to the business case process personnel.

Is the hunt effective?

Hunts may lose their effectiveness over time, and a determination of focusing resources on an activity may divert from other essential Hunting priorities. There are several reasons a hunt may lose its effectiveness or further need to be pursued:

- The creation of a rule covering the same activity may address the threat
- Completed patching against a known vulnerability may partially or mitigate the need for the hunt
- Improved automated tools or policies may also reduce the threat
- The determination that there is no longer an active threat in the IT environment.

Hunting can consume a significant amount of time, and analysts must ensure that their resources remain focused on fundamental and active threats. When a CTI analyst determines that a hunt can no longer provide effective results, documentation of the reasoning must be included in the MTHDB to retire the hunt.

Characteristics of a Successful Hunt Mission

A successful hunt occurs when the threat is identified, isolated, and prevented from conducting its mission. Furthermore, threat patterns are captured, business cases are generated, and the likelihood of any future exploitation by the threat is greatly minimized for any future win.

Event/Incident Outputs

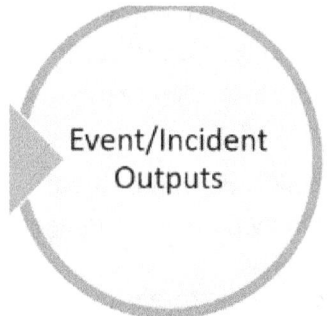

Event/Incident Outputs

Based on the outcome of the hunt, an analyst will document the results within the MTHDB. The products (reports) will be distributed as inputs to the IR function or business case development processes and provide necessary feedback to improve the analytical information provided by the CTI function.

Incident Response
If the hunt began from information collected from an IR function, providing feedback to that team helps improve its output. The IR team will be notified immediately following the verification of a malicious event in an information system or network.

Business Case Development
Upon determination that a high-fidelity, repeatable search helps detect anomalous or malicious activity, the logic will be delivered to the business case development process for creating or modifying current automated rules.

Cyber Threat Intelligence (CTI)
If the hunt began from the CTI function's information, providing feedback to that team helps improve their analysis. The Hunting process provides input relative to the provided intelligence, including the results of the hunt. It also supports the Hunting by determining whether additional information must continue and whether any information gained from the hunt could lead to other and useable intelligence. Any such additional intelligence would directly contribute to a CTI intelligence product or report's value and improvement.

Hunting Request (Externally focused): A pure Hunting request is typically focused on outside threats detected or anticipated based upon IOCs. This includes actual threats to operations within the agency's IT environment.

The following flowchart shows the *Hunting request* workflow.

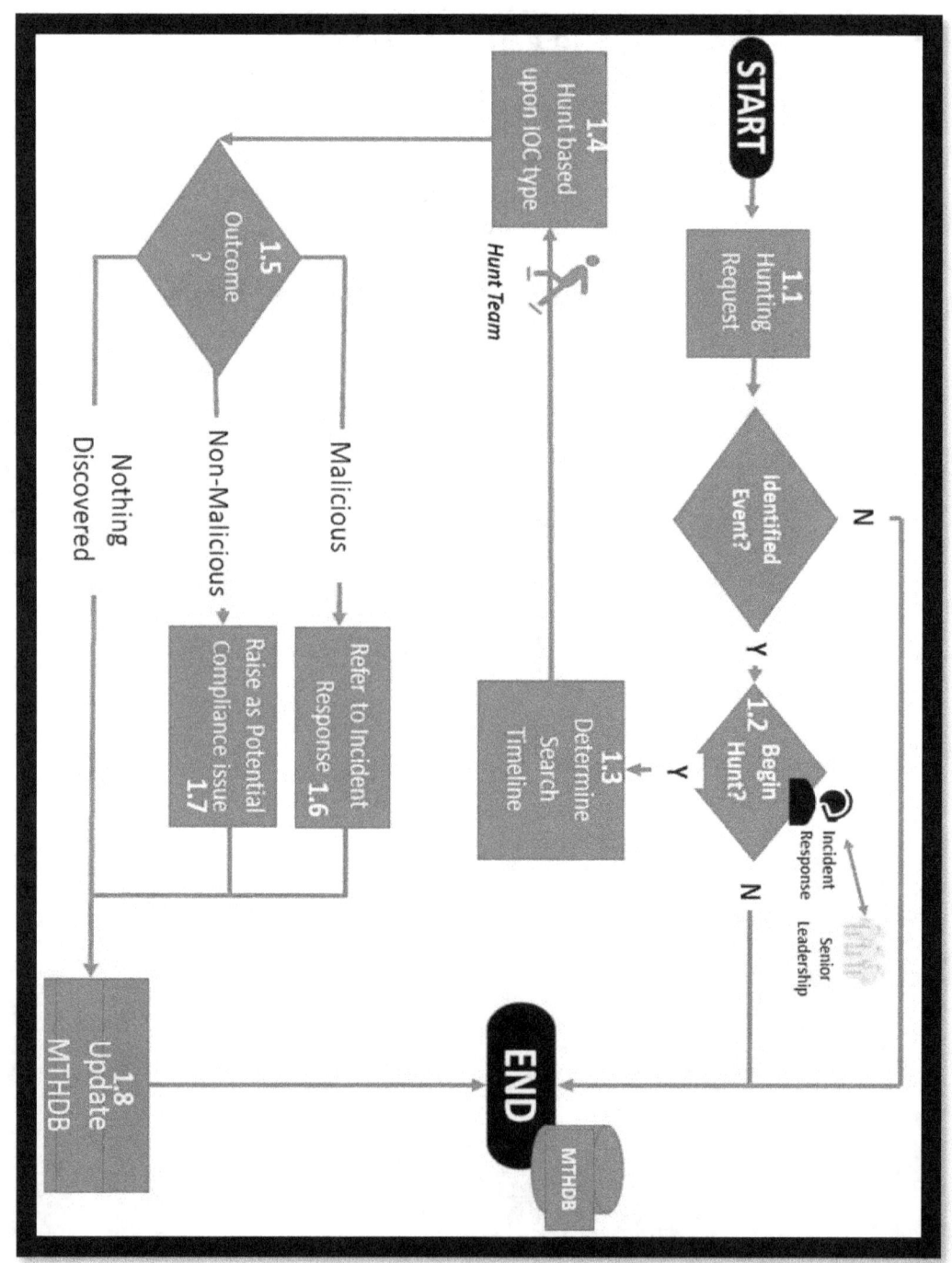

The Hunting Request Workflow Diagram

Roadmap Details

Hunting – Responsibility-Accountability-Consulted-Information (RACI) Matrix

1.1			Hunting Request
Input			Trigger Events: One of the following reactive or proactive triggers will prompt the initiation of the Hunting request process:
			• **Cyber Threat Intelligence:** IOCs provided by the CTI function identify internally/externally sourced, for example, Communities of Interest (CoI), Government Partners, Law Enforcement, etc.
			• **Business Case Development:** Feedback on a rule creation request received by the business case development process determined that a hunt would be appropriate based upon input.
			• **Incident Response:** IOCs provided by an IR function as part of, or resulting from, incident response activities.
RACI	R	Hunting Team	Responsible for analyzing the Hunt request and determining whether relevant details have been received to evaluate the request.
	A	Hunting Team Lead	Accountable to ensure that the Hunt request is given proper consideration and analysis.
	C	Trigger Source(s)	Consulted to provide full context regarding the hunt.
	I	Trigger	Informed of the next stage of analysis.

		Source(s)
Details		Hunting teams analyze a Hunt request made by the trigger source(s) and determine if there is appropriate information to evaluate the Hunt request.
Output		Hunting request requiring evaluation

1.2			Begin Hunting?	
Input			Hunting request requiring evaluation	
RACI	R	Hunting Team	Responsible for analyzing the Hunt request and determining whether to initiate a hunt.	
	A	Hunting Team Lead	Accountable to ensure that the Hunt request is given proper consideration and analysis.	
	C	Trigger Source(s)	Consulted to provide full context regarding the hunt.	
	I	Trigger Source(s)	Informed of the next stage of analysis.	

Details	The Hunting team evaluates the Hunt request and determines whether to initiate a hunt in coordination with IR personnel. The following criteria are used to determine if a hunt is to be initiated immediately or if further evaluation is required from an input source:

Cyber Threat Intelligence

Watchlists

The CTI team maintains access to various sources of intelligence feeds that provide high confidence for identified IOCs. Current whitelisted sources include, for example, iSight Threat Intelligence®.

The Hunting team initiates a hunt based upon indicators received from a threat intelligence source. (*Again, in coordination and at the direction of the IR team*).

IOC - Recommendation to Hunt

The CTI function will provide IOCs to the Hunting team and issue a recommendation to hunt when a moderate-to-high level of analyst confidence is obtained based upon established local thresholds and SOPs.

IOC – No Recommendation to Hunt

The CTI function will periodically provide IOCs to the IR team that does not include a recommendation to hunt when a low-to-moderate level of analyst confidence is obtained.

The Hunting team MAY perform further evaluation when an IOC with no recommendation to hunt is received from the CTI function.

Business Case Development

The business case development function may periodically provide IOCs and complementary courses of action to the Hunting team. This may result in a new rule request development effort. This is based upon recommendation and approval by the IR team where the business case (also called a "use case" or "vignette"[11]) development function deems a hunt may be appropriate.

The Hunting team performs further evaluation when an IOC hunt execution order is received. *(An example of a Threat Hunting Execution Order can be found in Appendix E).*

Copy _ of _ Copies

Organization/Unit:_____
Date:_____

THREAT HUNTING EXECUTION ORDER (#000001-2020-A)

References:
- **Network Topology Diagram: (See Annex A)**
- **Privileged User Password List (See Annex B)**
- **Contact Numbers (See Annex C)**
- **Cyber Deception Plan (See Annex D)**
- **Threat Assessment Report (See Annex E)**

Time Zone Used (☐ Z(GMT)):_____

1. **TYPE HUNT:** ☐ **HUNT** (EXTERNAL THREAT) ☐ **BASE HUNT** (INTERNAL)
   ☐ **BASE HUNT** (AD HOC/RECON) ☐ **HUNT** (EXERCISE)

2. ☐ **IMMEDIATE TASK:** ☐ Stop ☐ Confirm attribution
   ☐ Divert (Cyber-Deception Plan [CDP])_ ☐ Quarantine

3. ALLOCATED TIME: _____

---

[11] The terms "use case" or "vignette" are derived from the specialty area of Program Management (PM). Further information about the development of "business cases" may be found at many PM websites to include, for example, the Program Management Institute (PMI) at https://www.pmi.org/

Incident Response

The IR function may direct an IOC hunt as part of, or resulting from, incident response activities.

The Hunting team initiates a hunt anytime an IOC or other intelligence regarding threat activities are received from recognized intelligence or support activities. The Hunting team will begin a hunt in the direction of the IR function.

The Hunting team uses the following evaluation criteria to determine if a hunt should be initiated or if further evaluation of a Hunting request is required:

IOC Criteria	Factors that Support Hunting Initiation
Source	• Source has a history of providing high-confidence indicators.
Ease of Search	• The capability exists to search for the specific type and format of IOC.
Relevance	• The IOC is associated with malicious activity targeting industry peers or other relevant groups. • The IOC is related to technologies, applications, systems, etc., that are currently deployed.
Exposure	• The IOC is associated with malicious activity exploiting known vulnerabilities that exist within the IT environment. • The infection vector of the associated malicious activity is related and relevant to the regular activities or its users (e.g., watering hole attacks on popular public websites).
Existing Coverage	• Existing deployed security solutions are confirmed or unlikely to have detection rules for the IOC.
Impact	• The IOC is associated with a high-impact activity that may cause significant compromise to information or systems (e.g., Advance Persistent Threats[12] (APT), hacktivism, remote access tools, credential harvesters, etc.)

---

[12] APTs are typically nation-state cyber-activities supported by a nation. The top 3 major countries are China, Russia, and Iran, that specifically target US federal agencies and companies.

1.3			Determine Search Timelines
Input			Initiation of a new hunt
RACI	R	IR Team Lead	Responsible for analyzing the IOC and available supporting information to determine the appropriate search timeline. *The IR Team will determine the approximate amount of time and resources to ensure proper coverage of the Hunting activity and those rules for Hunting timeline extension, typically, with the senior agency or corporate leadership approval.*
	A	Hunting Team Lead	Accountable to ensure that the hunt timeline is appropriately scoped, monitored, and met.
	C	Trigger Source(s)	Consulted to provide input on the hunt timeline.
	I	Trigger Source(s)	Informed of the next stage of analysis.
Details			The IR team determines the search timeline for the hunt based on the following criteria for each respective input source:

Details (continued)

Cyber Threat Intelligence

Watchlist
The search timeline for an IOC originating from a threat intelligence feed should align with the recommendation issued by the IOC source. A default of a 🔆 thirty (30) days[13] should be used if the IOC source has suggested no recommended search timeline.

---

[13] Timelines are suggested and may be modified according to the availability of resources and risk management direction within local policy or procedure documents; these are provided as general guides only.

	IOC - Recommendation to Hunt The search timeline for an IOC with a recommendation to hunt from the CTI function should be determined by the CTI function and included with the Hunting request. *IOC –Recommendation to Hunt Has Not Been Included* 💡 A default of thirty (30) days should be used for an IOC originating from the CTI function with no recommendation to hunt included. **Business Case Development** 💡 A default of thirty (30) days should be used for an IOC originating from the case development function. **Incident Response** The search timeline for an IOC from the IR function should be determined by the IR function and included with the Hunting request.	
Output	Hunting request search timeline(s) is established.	

1.4		Hunt Based upon IOC Type	
Input		Hunting request with established search timeline	
RACI	R	Hunting Team Analyst	Responsible for performing the Hunt.
	A	Hunting Team Lead	Accountable to ensure that the hunt is appropriately performed.
	C	Hunting Team	Consulted regarding the hunt methodology as required.

	I	Hunting Team	Informed of the hunt details to ensure coordination.
Details		The Hunting team analysts perform the hunt based on the established search timelines and IOC types. The following guidance is used to perform the hunt for each IOC type (all historical searches are to be limited to the established search timelines). If direct access to a security device is not feasible, interrogation of Security Information and Event Manager (SIEM) or a centralized log management system may be leveraged for hunting purposes.	

Hunting Guidance for IOC Types

IOC Type	
Email	Perform a search using the email security solution where the specific indicator (e.g., subject, sender, message body, etc.) matches the IOC.
File	Create a new indicator on, for example, FireEye HX® with one or more of the following file conditions (as applicable/available) that match the IOC: a. File path: *equal, contains,* or *matches* b. SHA-256[14]: *equal* c. File size (in bytes): *equal*

IP Address	1. Perform a search for:
	
	  a. Successful or denied firewall connections where the source or destination Internet Protocol (IP) address matches the IOC.
	
	  b. Successful or denied web proxy events where the source or destination IP address matches the IOC.
	
	  c. Intrusion Detection System (IDS)/Intrusion Prevention System (IPS) events where the source or destination IP address matches the IOC.
	
	  d. Successful or denied web application firewall events where the source or destination IP address matches the IOC.
	
	2. Create a new indicator with one or more of the following Network Connection conditions (as applicable/available) that match the IOC:

---

[14] SHA-256 is the federally recommended hashing standard. Older versions, such as MD-5 is highly-breakable and is no longer in use by most major corporations due to its current vulnerabilities.

	a. Local or remote (destination) IP addresses: *equal* b. Local or remote (destination) ports: equal, is *greater than, is less than*, and *is between*.
Network (string, traffic pattern, user agent)	1. Review externally facing, perimeter, and internal IDS logs (as applicable) where the specific network artifact indicator matches the IOC. 2. Perform a search of web and application logs on vulnerable externally facing systems where the specific network artifact indicator matches the IOC. 3. Perform a search on any existing Web Application Firewalls (WAF) on vulnerable externally facing systems where the specific network artifact indicator matches the IOC.
Registry Key	Create a new indicator in, for example, FireEye HX® that matches the IOC.
URL	1. Perform a search for web proxy events where the Uniform Resource Locator (URL) matches the IOC. 2. Create a new indicator with the following Domain Name Service (DNS) Lookup condition that matches the IOC: a. DNS lookup: *equal, contains,* or *matches*
SIEM	Instead of analysts having direct access to the security devices, interrogation of SIEM or centralized log management system will be leveraged for Hunting.
Output	*Completed Hunt*

1.5			Outcome
Input			Completed Hunt
RACI	R	Hunting Team Analyst	Responsible for ensuring that any required referral occurs depending on the hunt outcome.
	A	Hunting Team Lead	Accountable to ensure that any required referral occurs depending on the hunt outcome.
	C	Trigger Source(s)	Consulted regarding the hunt outcome before referral or Hunting process completion.
	I	Trigger Source(s)	Informed of the hunt outcome
Details			The Hunt concludes with one of the following three outcomes:

Details

The Hunt concludes with one of the following three outcomes:

Something Discovered: Malicious

An active or historic compromise that may currently or have previously placed its assets or its **data**[15] at risk; Discovered during the Hunting activity.

Something Discovered: Non-Malicious

Violation(s) of acceptable use or organizational policies discovered during the hunt.

---

[15] **Data** is the main item within any network that should be specifically protected especially if is of a sensitive or restricted nature; modern-day cybersecurity protections are focused on data protection.

		Nothing Discovered
		No indication of active compromise or behavior violating acceptable use or organizational policies was discovered.
Output		Completed Hunting

1.6			Refer to Incident Response
Input			Completed Hunting with malicious findings.
RACI	R	Hunting Team Analyst	Responsible for ensuring that all required information and context are referred to as the appropriate IR function.
	A	Hunting Team Lead	Accountable for ensuring that all required information and context are referred to the IR function.
	C	Incident Response Team	Consulted regarding the referral process.
	I	Incident Response Team	Informed of the malicious finding.
Details			All information regarding the hunt and the malicious finding's details are compiled by the Hunting team analyst and referred to the IR function.
Output			Referral to the affected IR function.

1.7	Raise as a Potential Compliance Issue[16]		
Input	Completed hunt with non-malicious finding		
RACI	**R**	Hunting Team Analyst	Responsible for ensuring that all required information and context are handed to the relevant internal function(s) for escalation as a *compliance issue*.
	A	Hunting Team Lead	Accountable for ensuring that all required information and context are handed to the relevant internal function(s) for escalation as a compliance issue.
	C	Relevant Internal Function(s)	Consulted regarding the referral process.
	I	Relevant Internal Function(s)	Informed of the non-malicious finding.
Details	All information regarding the hunt and the details of the non-malicious finding is compiled by the Hunting team analyst [CTI analyst] and referred to the relevant internal function(s) to include senior leadership for escalation as a compliance issue.		
Output	Refer to the relevant internal function(s).		

---

[16] Some businesses and agencies identify "best practice" violations as a compliance issue. *It is not.* Failures of best practice may include, for example, weak passwords or leaving smart cards unattended. Such failures must be captured and enforceable through acceptable use or like business policies are Human Resource sanctioned policies and laws for the punishment of an individual.

1.8			Update MTHDB
Input			Completed Hunting.
RACI	R	Hunting Team Analyst	Responsible for ensuring the MTHDB is updated with all required information regarding the completed hunt and outcome.
	A	Hunting Team Lead	Accountable for ensuring the MTHDB is updated with all required information regarding the completed hunt and outcome.
	C	N/A	N/A
	I	Hunting Team Trigger Source(s)	Informed of the completed hunt and outcome.
Details			The Hunting team analyst updates the MTHDB with all required information regarding the completed hunt and outcome and notifies the trigger source(s) that the hunt has been completed, and provides the results.
Output			**Completed Hunting**

Base Hunting (Internally focused)

Base hunting is typically used to monitor compliance and "insider threat" activities. It can be initiated based upon known or suspected activities from within the agency or used to conduct ad hoc inspection of individuals and sub-agencies that may be in non-compliance with corporate or agency acceptable use policies and procedures.

The following flowchart shows the detailed flow of the *Base* **Hunting** workflow.

When does a hunt become a base hunt?

- *A standard hunt, focused on external intrusions, becomes a base hunt once a determination that a threat is an employee, contractor, or entity of the company or agency with general (a standard user) or privileged (system or database administrators) users accessing the IT environment, and are engaged in unauthorized activities.*

Unauthorized activities are defined by an Acceptable Use Policy (AUP). Unauthorized use may include accessing gambling, pornographic sites, etc., in violation of the AUP. In the case of personnel identified as having elevated or privileged access, such activities as accessing data, files, or locations not authorized as part of their duty role or assignment may violate the AUP.

A hunt may quickly become a base hunt once better identification and attribution of the individual are determined.

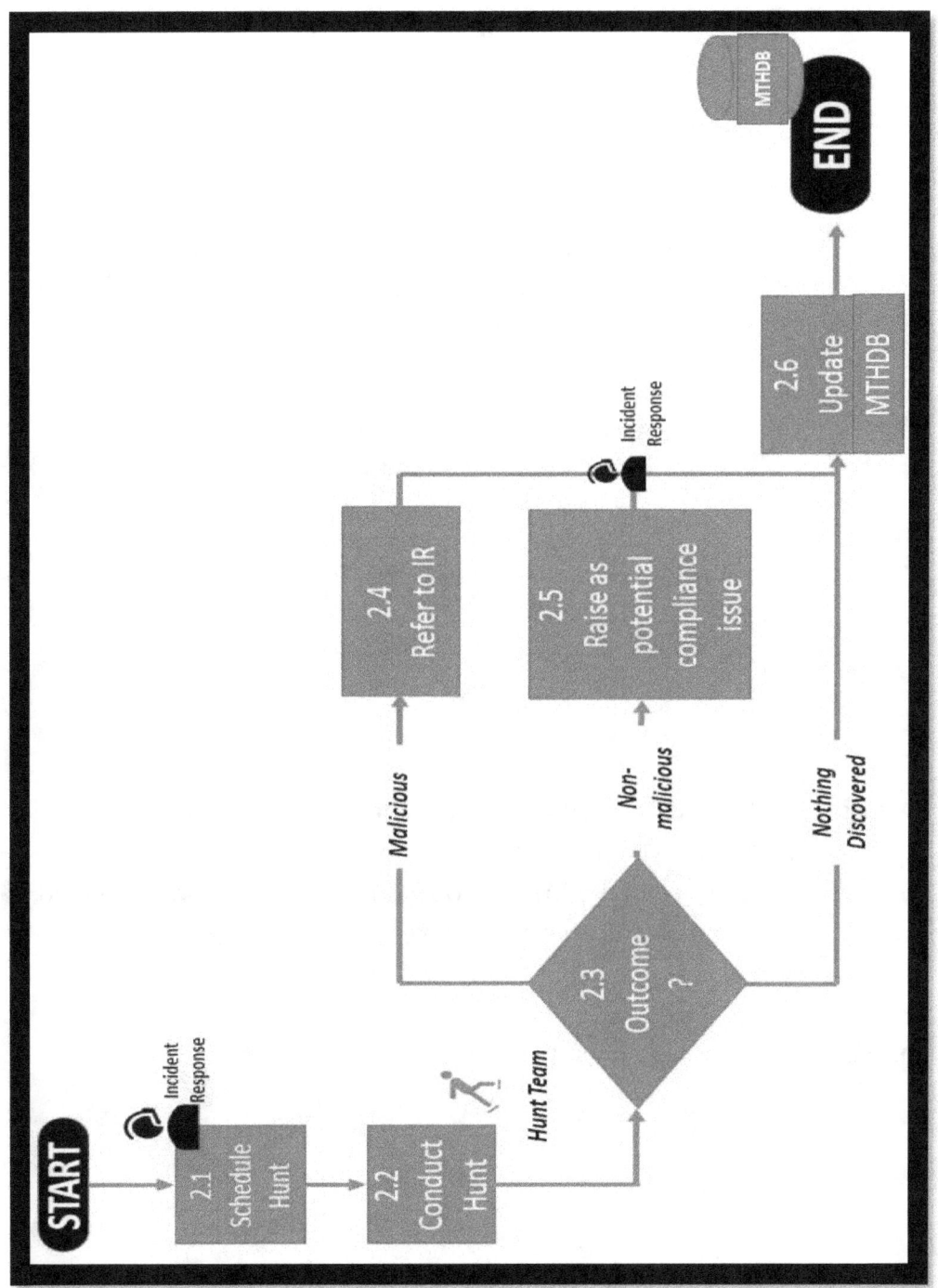

Base Hunting Workflow Diagram

Base Hunting - RACI Matrix

2.1			Schedule Hunt
Input			Base Hunting is triggered by "hunt schedule.[17]"
RACI	**R**	Hunting Team	Responsible for maintaining an awareness of the hunt schedule and performing time management accordingly.
	A	Hunting Team Lead	Accountable to ensure that the hunt schedule is being adhered to and that the required resources are appropriately managed.
	C	N/A	N/A
	I	N/A	N/A
Details			The base hunt schedule specifies the frequency that the base Hunting is to be performed. The next hunt run-date and time are recorded in the MTHDB. Upcoming base hunts will be added to the queue and assigned to an available Hunting team member.
Output			Base Hunting queued for action.

---

[17] A "hunt schedule" is used for pre-planned base hunt inspections of the agency's IT environment that is coordinated between IR and Hunt personnel. It is typically restricted to personnel with a need-to-only purpose.

2.2			Conduct Hunting
Input			Base Hunting queued to be performed.
RACI	R	Hunting Team Analyst	Responsible for performing the hunt.
	A	Hunting Team Lead	Accountable to ensure that the hunt is appropriately performed.
	C	Hunting Team	Consulted regarding the hunt methodology as required.
	I	Hunting Team	Informed of the hunt details to ensure coordination.
Details			The Hunting team analyst performs the hunt based on the hunt activities and established search timelines as determined in the MTHDB.
Output			**Hunting completed**

2.3			Outcome
Input		Hunting completed	
RACI	R	Hunting Team Analyst	Responsible for ensuring that any required referral occurs depending on the final hunt outcome.
	A	Hunting Team Lead	Accountable to ensure that any required referral occurs depending on the final hunt outcome.
	C	N/A	N/A
	I	N/A	N/A

Details	The Hunting concludes with one of the following three outcomes:

Something Discovered: Malicious

Active or historic compromise, which may currently or have previously placed, its assets, or its information at risk, discovered during the hunt.

Something Discovered: Non-Malicious

Violation(s) of acceptable use or organizational policies discovered during the hunt.

Nothing Discovered

No indication of active compromise or behavior violating acceptable use or organizational policies.

Output	Completed Hunting

2.4			Refer to Incident Response
Input			Completed Hunting with malicious finding
RACI	R	Hunting Team Analyst	Responsible for ensuring that all required information and context are handed to the appropriate IR function.
	A	Hunting Team Lead	Accountable for ensuring that all required information and context are handed to the appropriate IR function.
	C	Incident Response Team	Consulted regarding the referral process.
	I	Incident Response Team	Informed of malicious findings
Details			All information regarding the hunt and the malicious finding's details are compiled by the Hunting team analyst and provided to the affected IR function.
Output			Refer to the IR function.

2.5			Raise as a Potential Compliance Issue
Input			Completed Hunting with non-malicious findings.
RACI	R	Hunting Team Analyst	Responsible for ensuring that all required information and context is provided to the relevant internal function(s)[18] for escalation as a compliance issue.
	A	Hunting Team Lead	Accountable for ensuring that all required information and context is given to the relevant internal function(s) for escalation as a compliance issue.
	C	Relevant Internal Function(s)	Consulted regarding referred to process.
	I	Relevant Internal Function(s)	Informed of the non-malicious finding.
Details			All information regarding the hunt and the details of the non-malicious finding is compiled by the Hunting team analyst and provided to the relevant internal function(s) for escalation as a compliance issue.
Output			Handoff to relevant internal function(s)

---

[18] This could include senior leadership, an individual's direct supervisor, or Human Resources (HR) to begin disciplinary actions and documentation requirements.

2.6			Update MTHDB
Input			Completed Hunting
RACI	**R**	Hunting Team Analyst	Responsible for ensuring the MTHDB is updated with all required information regarding the completed hunt and outcome.
	A	Incident Response with Hunting Team Lead	Accountable for ensuring the MTHDB is updated with all required information regarding the completed hunt and outcome.
	C	N/A	N/A
	I	Hunting Team	Informed of the completed hunt and outcome.
Details			The hunting team analyst updates the MTHDB with all required information regarding the completed hunt and outcome.
Output			**Completed Hunting process**

Roles and Responsibilities for the MHTDB

The CTI Analysts are ultimately responsible for updating the MTHDB. It may take the form of a relational database or a more advanced information-sharing platform, for example, Microsoft's Sharepoint®. It is the determination of company or agency leadership the resourcing to create, maintain, and support the long-term viability of an effective MTHDB.

The Threat Hunting team's role is to collect the data and inputs of both a qualitative and quantitative nature to create a good database. Information is provided to the CTI Analysts during and after operations; however, updating the MTHDB should always be committed to the CTI team.

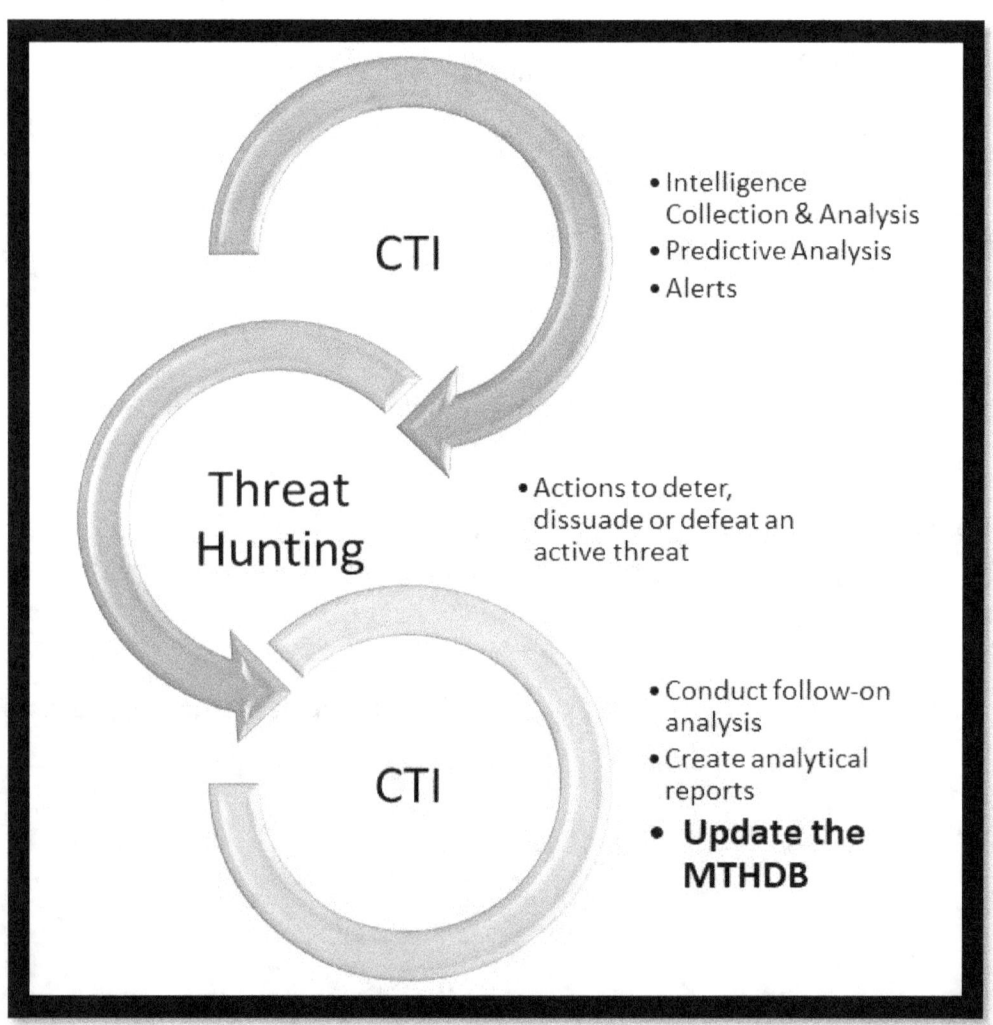

The Role of Metrics

A Hunting program should provide weekly, monthly, and annual metrics to corporate or agency leadership. The weekly metrics provide information regarding threats reviewed during the past week and any anticipated activities based upon sound analytical tradecraft, and IOCs are seen active within the infrastructure. (Also, see Appendix C, *"Can the Human Poet Bring Value to Predictive Analysis?"* This is a discussion on how human experts can work with growing data analytic science capabilities and the value of cybersecurity analysis soon.)

The monthly metrics report should provide trends and resource utilization. Patterns should be connected to frequent malicious intrusions and external intelligence sources cooperative with a part of the critical infrastructure. Annual metrics provide a holistic view of the Hunting program to ensure it:

- Meets business objectives
- Identifies additional resourcing
- Delineates cooperative information sharing activities within the infrastructure for which an agency belongs.

Weekly Metrics

Weekly metrics reporting for the Hunting program will occur in a weekly status report. Weekly metrics include the outcomes of hunts completed during the previous seven days. Metrics should include IOCs identified and resolved during the prior week. It should also include final analytic reports created and disseminated to both internal divisions and external partners to include corporate stakeholders and state and federal government entities charged with cybersecurity oversight.

Monthly Metrics

Monthly metrics for the hunting program will be reported and delivered during each calendar month's first whole week. The monthly metrics report will provide metrics regarding hunting program functions, including:

- Hunts conducted by attack lifecycle

- Hunt outcomes
- Hunts transferred to business case development
- Hunts escalated to the Incident Response team

Annual Metrics

Annual metrics will provide a view of where the hunting program has improved over the year and aligned with the companies' or agencies' strategic goals. It should also present any Hunting program's issues, such as a lack of necessary tools or data sources to complete effective Hunting operations.

Qualitative versus Quantitative Metrics

The best metrics are those that can:

1. **Be measurable or quantified, and**
2. **Provide value to the company or agency**

Metrics should be derived by the value created by CTI and Hunting personnel responding (time factor) and effectively (intrusion caught and minimized) mitigating threats to the IT environment. No metrics are ever a certainty for security but provide the needed insight to managerial oversight, not just within the area of cybersecurity protection and response.

⚠️ *Several measures can be used; however, they do not recommend the Risk Matrix approach alone. The risk matrix introduces too many unsubstantiated unknowns and should be deferred to more meaningful metrics built from the business's operational needs and necessities.*

The Fallacy of The Risk Reporting Matrix

The Risk Reporting Matrix (RRM) is a classic means to characterize risk levels (Under Secretary of Defense for Acquisition, Technology, and Logistics, 2006) to programs and initiatives to include the Defense department's risks, program management efforts, and cybersecurity community. Its representation is simplistic, but its implications are far-reaching. Hayden (2010) and Hubbard and Seiersen (2016) have significant issues with current methodologies used to assess risk across industries, but cybersecurity specifically. "They are a failure. They do not work" (Hubbard & Seiersen, 2016, p. 14); the RRM is one of their specific concerns.

The RRM requires users to apply subjective labels to a typical 5x5 matrix; Figure 1 provides an example of an RRM (University of Melbourne, 2018) where the "likelihood" or probability is on the vertical and "consequence" or impact are across the horizontal axes. Users are to: "[d]evelop probability [emphasis added] and consequence scales by allocating thresholds across the WBS [Work Breakdown Structure]…" (Under Secretary of Defense for Acquisition, Technology, and Logistics, 2006, p. 14), but they are not provided the back-end methodologies or mathematics to derive such calculations. The RRM was never designed or defined as a quantitative risk measure (Project Management Skills, 2010). Practitioners of Risk Management (RM) and RRM reporting recipients have assumed it is founded upon solid analyses and statistics; they have unfortunately been wrong.

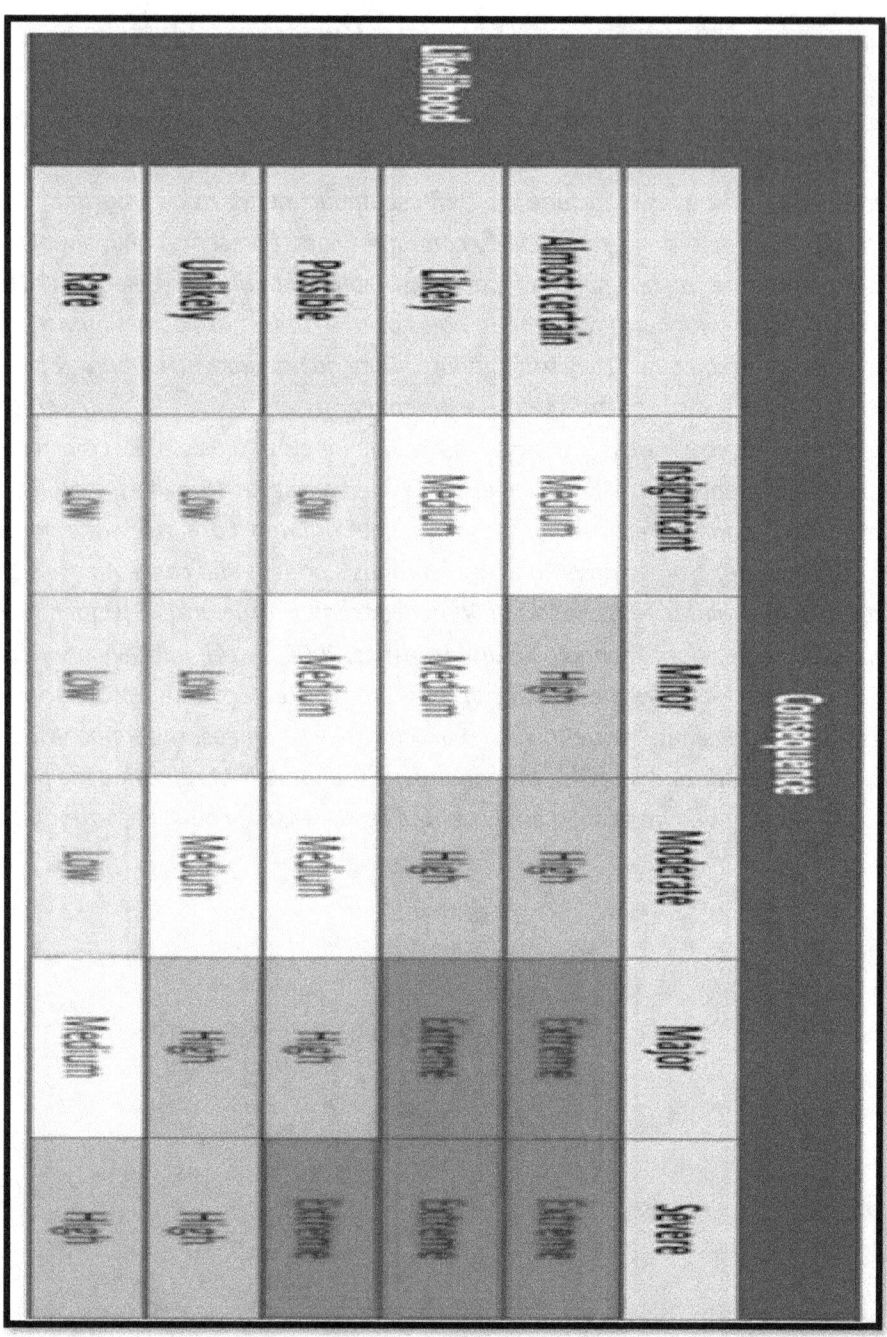

Figure 1. Health & Safety – Risk matrix and definitions. Adapted from "Risk Assessment Methodology" by the University of Melbourne, p. 11, Copyright 2018 by the University of Melbourne.

While there is seldom one solution to any problem, the initial solution is eliminating the RRM. While its abandonment is fundamental, it would remove the interpretation that users' objective mathematical precision by users that the RRM is ideal in the identification and management of risk. "Our somewhat naïve definition of risk in the context of IT security is mirrored by the lack of rigor we tend to demonstrate in measuring it" (Hayden, 2010, p. 9). The elimination of the RRM is the first step to improving our ability to assess cybersecurity risk better because it gives a false sense of evaluating risk.

Hubbard and Seiersen (2016) provide one significantly accepted commercial approach. They introduce the initial foundation of establishing a "quantitative risk assessment" (Hubbard & Seiersen, 2016, p. 35) process. This method relies on individuals' subjective expertise within the field of cybersecurity and leads to actual mathematical output. They begin with replacing the subjective RRM terms as the metrics of "high," "medium," and "low." They replace them with new probabilities and dollar impacts based upon expert knowledge. They present a modern means to include expert knowledge and experience to formulate an improved solution.

This answer portends an ongoing refinement and provides the framework to progress predictive analytics needed to improve the field of cybersecurity RM. Hubbard and Seiersen's (2016) process identifies the anticipated risks by the Subject Matter Expert (SME), who define over a period that the risk may occur. This process includes assigning subjective probability scoring of 0-100% to become part of the SME's overall prediction. The next step is to give an actual range of monetary cost if the event were to occur within a 90% Confidence Interval (CI); this bounds the estimate within a range of a 90% probability whether a risk occurs, and an assessment of a business cost range is additionally included (Hubbard & Seiersen, 2016).

The final step is the total of all expert predictions that are averaged and become the foundation of both a final probability (e.g., a 65% likelihood) and uncertainty (i.e., within the established 90% CI of this methodology) process refinement (Hubbard & Seiersen, 2016). This becomes the critical basis of better risk predictions, as historically found in Sir Francis Galton's experiment in 1906. Galton collected individual "expert" predictions in this experiment averaged them to forecast a slaughtered cow's actual weight within one pound of its actual weight (Tetlock & Gardner, 2016).

These combined solutions are substantive and optimal for the progress of improving the state of cybersecurity RM. It would move the state of predictive cybersecurity RM to better than a dart-throwing chimpanzee (Tetlock & Gardner, 2016).

It would remove the RRM that introduces a dangerous flaw in the rational belief that it represents quantified certainty. Hubbard and Seiersen (2016) added the next critical step—to instead use the experts focused on better confined and probabilistic evaluations and predictions. Thus, the subjective expertise of individuals "bridges" us closer to a more objective means to assess and predict risk.

Other solutions are more heavily mathematically based, such as the use of Monte Carlo and regression models. These lend themselves to more objective outcomes; however, they do not leverage the accumulation of SMEs' knowledge. Mathematical models may be better but are devoid of human knowledge, experience, and intuition that can identify the elements of uncertainty and surprise that are more difficult to introduce into a mathematical algorithm. While none of this reduces cost, time, or convenience, they supplement our ability to predict better the consequences of risk to the user, agency, or company.

There is seldom a single best solution. There are more typically optimal solutions. The more answers introduced to mitigate a problem, the higher the chance of successfully solving the overall situation. The elimination of the RRM is necessitated not because it is a wrong model but because its presence introduces a false sense of security and certainty. Unless its use implements actual mathematical rigor, it must be retired immediately.

Finally, Hubbard and Seiersen's (2016) work is essential to bring predictive analysis aligned more with accepted mathematical norms. This includes the ability of SMEs to attain an objective outcome. It would advance cybersecurity RM and eliminate the lack of real objectivity hidden behind a false and historical acceptance of the flawed RRM.

References for "The Fallacy of The Risk Reporting Matrix"

Hayden, L. (2010). *IT security metrics: A practical framework for measuring security & protecting data.* New York: McGraw Hill.

Hubbard, D., & Seiersen, R. (2016). *How to measure anything in cybersecurity risk.* Hoboken, NJ: John Wiley & sons.

Project Management Skills. (2010, September 5). *Qualitative risk analysis and assessment.* Retrieved from Project Management Skills: https://www.project-management-skills.com/qualitative-risk-analysis.html

Tetlock, P., & Gardner, D. (2016). *Superforecasting: The art and science of prediction.* New York: Random House.

Under Secretary of Defense for Acquisition, Technology, and Logistics. (2006, August). *Risk management guide for DOD acquisition.* Retrieved from Office of the Under Secretary of Defense for Acquisition, Technology, and Logistics: https://www.acq.osd.mil/damir/documents/DAES_2006_RISK_GUIDE.pdf

Under Secretary of Defense for Acquisition, Technology, and Logistics. (2017, January). *Risk, issue, and opportunity management guide for defense acquisition programs.* Retrieved from Office of the Under Secretary of Defense for Acquisition, Technology, and Logistics: https://www.acq.osd.mil/se/docs/2017-rio.pdf

University of Melbourne. (2018, May). *Risk assessment methodology.* Retrieved from University of Melbourne: https://safety.unimelb.edu.au/__data/assets/pdf_file/0007/1716712/health-and-safety-risk-assessment-methodology.pdf

PART III - Tactical Activities

C-THP Tactical Methodology

The following chapter provides a detailed depiction of the procedures for a "Hunting Mission Program." It is centered upon the four areas that modestly parallel the Intelligence Community's Intelligence Lifecycle. The CTI and Hunting Team analysts will work cooperatively throughout the C-THP Methodology. IR personnel may also play a role and will act as approval of any current or continued action against any known or suspected occurrence, event, or incident.

An effective Hunting Mission Program relies upon the following four areas:

1. **Designate**
2. **Acquire**
3. **Analyze**
4. **Reporting**

Designate — Determine the physical and virtual boundaries of the hunt

Acquire — Conduct technical scans of the environment to determine malicious activities

Analyze — Provide predictive analysis of malicious actors current and future likely activities

Reporting — Identify impacts and disseminate analysis throughout the organization to reduce future harm

The C-THP Methodology begins with defining the boundaries that need to be identified as part of hunt activities. *Designate* identifies all IT hardware, software, network assets, etc., that likely are directly affected by known or suspected malicious activities. Without a clear understanding of boundaries, analytic resources may be inadvertently diverted or distracted by not defining the effort's scope.

Acquire is identical to the collection phase of the Intelligence Lifecycle, as described earlier. In this phase, CTI analysts conduct technical scans of the targeted IT environment to determine malicious activities. Various scans are used to detect unauthorized port access, identify types of injected malware, use IOC databases to assess potential threats, etc. Acquire gathers all relevant data and facts around an event or incident for organizational action and IR alerts to senior and government officials as required by policy or law.

In the *Analyze* phase, Hunting team members, in close coordination with CTI personnel, determine the who, what, where, etc., factors to identify attribution of the attack and whether the attack rises to the level of a reportable event or incident. Analyze is a continual process that develops intelligence reports and offers predictive intelligence to the organization and third-party cooperative businesses or agency members. Analyze provides critical (immediate), short-term (within 24 hours), and long-term (typically monthly) analytical reports to members of both the technical and non-technical personnel of the organization; this phase is identical within the Intelligence Lifecycle.

Finally, **Reporting** identifies impacts on the IT environment and supports resourcing identification and demands where senior leaders must play a decisive role. Reporting also ensures the quality review of reporting and provides timely dissemination throughout the organization. Senior leaders are accountable for guaranteeing critical intelligence identification, and communications are timely to reduce especially malicious activities against the company or agency's infrastructure.

The following sections provide greater "tactical" clarity for the Hunting Team, CTI Analysts, IR personnel, and Senior Leaders. This more descriptive application of the Hunting teams' efforts begins with *Designate*.

Designate

The focus of the *Designate* phase is to develop a hypothesis. Formulate a hypothesis or hypotheses, as appropriate. The theory can be based on several different inputs, including:

- Internal use of business scenarios

- Threat exposure checks (Base Hunts)[19]
- Incident response activities
- CTI

The hypothesis should consider:

- **Source confidence** – the source has a history of proving high-confidence indicators. Ratings may be qualitative, for example, *high-confidence, reliable, questionable*, based upon the source's reputation. Quantitative measures can also be applied to include, for example, the use of Confidence Intervals (CI): *"The lead analyst is 90% confident the threat is Russian-backed organized crime unit out of Moscow with a CI of 10%."*
- **Expected ease of the search** – the capability exists to search for the specific type, indicators, and format of the IOC.
- **Target and searchable data of relevance** – The IOC is associated with malicious activity targeting, industry peers, or other relevant groups. The IOC may be related to technologies, applications, etc., that are currently deployed within the IT environment.
- **Known exposure** – The IOC is associated with malicious activity exploiting known vulnerabilities that exist in the environment. The IOC is also used to identify the attack vector of the malicious activity and determine whether it is related and relevant to normal operational activities.
- **Existing infrastructure and visibility** – Existing tools are confirmed to have visibility or detection capability for the specific IOC.
- **Potential impact** – The IOC is associated with the high-impact activity that may cause significant damage in the event of a compromise.

The hypothesis should also answer a basic set of standard questions that help scope and define the hunt.

- What are we looking for?

---

[19] A **base hunt**, or **threat exposure check**, is defined as a repeatable search based on analytical methodology which produces a low fidelity results (i.e., results that require analyst review and cannot be fully automated as a rule); these hunts will reside in the MHTDB.

- Where will we look?
- What do we expect to find or not find?
- Why are we looking for it?
- What will its presence or absence tell us?
- Who or what will consume the outputs?

After developing the hypothesis, the CTI analyst will next:

- Identify the target criteria
- Establish a timeframe and expected duration of the hunt in coordination with IR personnel.
- Identify execution resources and constraints
- Establish expected outcomes
- Communicate intent and scope to leadership and stakeholders

Metrics: The data fields that may provide value to technical and non-technical leadership may include:

- Case records
- Dates opened
- Expected start and end times

- Actual start time and end times
- Hypotheses
- Objective summaries
- Target criteria and supporting information
- Source or use case
- Stakeholder output
- Target IOCs

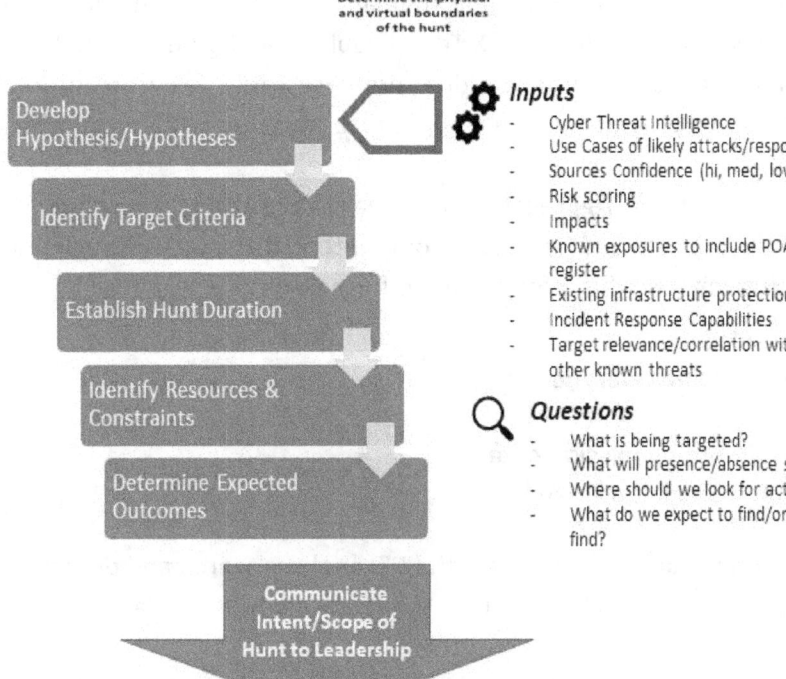

Designate

Determine the physical
and virtual boundaries
of the hunt

Develop
Hypothesis/Hypotheses

Identify Target Criteria

Establish Hunt Duration

Identify Resources &
Constraints

Determine Expected
Outcomes

Communicate
Intent/Scope of
Hunt to Leadership

Inputs
- Cyber Threat Intelligence
- Use Cases of likely attacks/responses
- Sources Confidence (hi, med, low)
- Risk scoring
- Impacts
- Known exposures to include POAM register
- Existing infrastructure protections
- Incident Response Capabilities
- Target relevance/correlation with other known threats

Questions
- What is being targeted?
- What will presence/absence signify?
- Where should we look for activity?
- What do we expect to find/or not find?

Data to be captured
- Case Record
- Hypothesis/hypotheses
- Date opened
- Source or Use case
- Objective summary
- Start/stop date/time
- Target found/forensics (IP addresses, MAC, etc.)
- Indicators of Compromise (IOC) correlation (correct, not correct, or new)

Figure 1. 'Designate' Workflow and Considerations

Acquire

The next area of the Hunting process is the _Acquire_ phase. This may also be referred to as the collection phase. The CTI analyst will access tools and data to begin collecting vital data to determine the level of intrusion and associated risks to the company or agency.

Access Tools and Data – Primary candidate tools may include, for example, Splunk®, FireEye HX®, the FireEye PX Tech-Enabler®, and other internal information and toolsets. This effort does not necessarily flow from internal tools; however, it should provide adequate support for forensic artifacts or other data log collections.

The CTI analysts will **Aggregate and Prepare Target Data**, to include IOCs, and determine whether the data is relevant or of interest. The analysts will primarily, but not exclusively, use this information to formulate:

- Specific IOCs
- CTI extracts and references
- IR data
- Previous Hunting mission data
- Environmental knowledge

Search infrastructure and data – the CTI analysts search and depending on the type of IOCs. The search will collect the following types of data:

- Domain names
- Hypertext Transfer Protocol (HTTP) methods and code
- Endpoint registry information
- Simple Mail Transfer Protocol (SMTP) Header data
- File names, paths, and types
- Hypertext Markup Language (HTML)/Java source code
- File sizes
- Uniform Resource Identifier (URI) strings
- Uniform Resource Locators (URL)
- Process names
- Source and destination ports and protocols
- File hashes
- Destination Internet Protocols (IP)
- Attachment names and hashes

- Byte counts (transferred)
- User-agent strings
- Attacker/Source IPs

Validate Completion of Searches – the *CTI analyst will validate the data* from the searches and answer the following:

- Is the target data searchable by the tools and the infrastructure?
- Did all searches from all sources complete as expected?
- Were searches completed within an acceptable timeframe?
- Were there any undesirable or unexpected results?
- Were there any outlier[20] ("black swan") concerns raised by the search? Should it be further monitored/reported?

The initial analysis is performed in a triage manner to determine if immediate or high-impact threats were detected and if so, those are escalated using the established IR Plan (IRP). The IR staff will be notified. If there are no findings, the CTI analyst then **Documents the Findings and Updates the Case Status**[21]. This will include updates to the MTHDB to support ongoing trend analysis efforts. Even events must become part of the MTHDB record because while the event may have been determined to be reportable, it may be a precursor of a future attack.[22]

Metrics: The data fields for compiling suggested potential metrics include:

- Initial analyses
- Actual and final correlated target data
- Infrastructure searched to include all hardware and software devices.
- High fidelity indicators further confirm the accuracy and completeness of any analytic reports, white papers, summaries, etc.
- Summary of search result successes and failures

---

[20] An outlier or "black swan" event in a low or unexpected occurrence based on past historical data and intelligence. While these are uncommon, they may highlight new and changing Tactics, Techniques and Procedures (TTP) by hackers.

[21] Reminder: The CTI Analyst is responsible for updating any records to include repositories, databases, and especially the MTHDB.

[22] Nation-states hackers may conduct low-level "probing" actions to identify weaknesses in corporate perimeters and networks. They are intended to ascertain the level of defensive complexity an environment may or may not have to future attack.

- Escalations to the IR team for additional resourcing or action

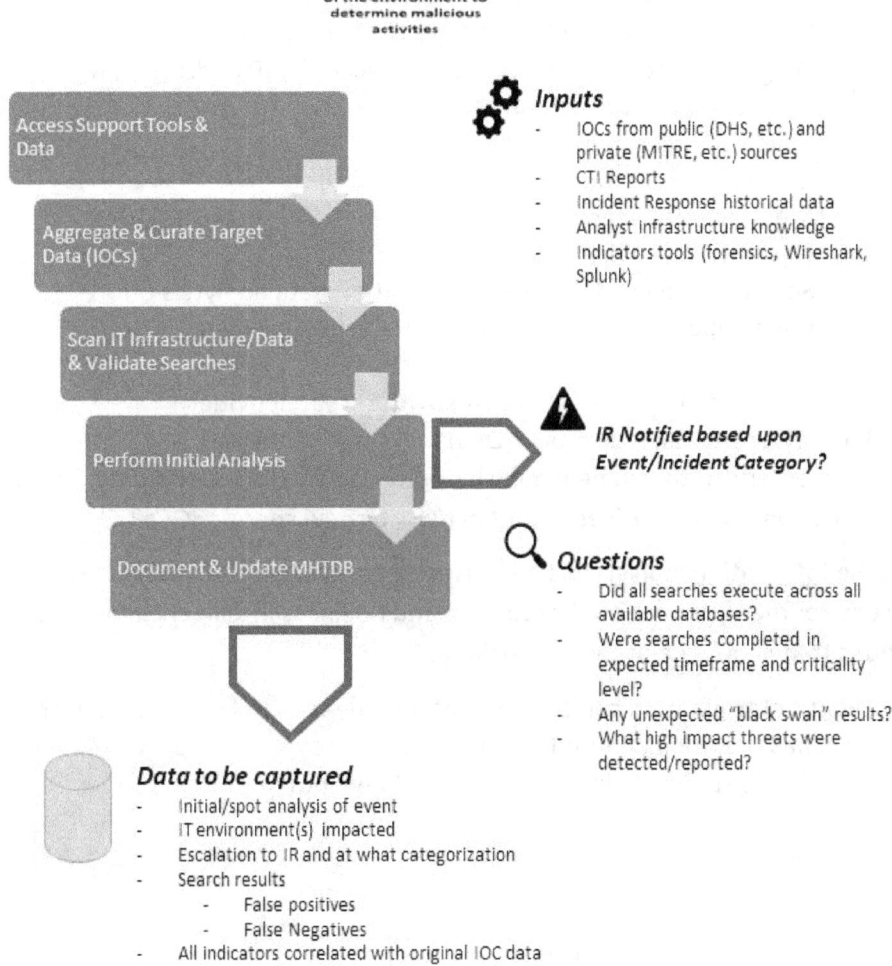

Acquire

Conduct technical scans of the environment to determine malicious activities

Access Support Tools & Data

Aggregate & Curate Target Data (IOCs)

Scan IT Infrastructure/Data & Validate Searches

Perform Initial Analysis

Document & Update MHTDB

Inputs
- IOCs from public (DHS, etc.) and private (MITRE, etc.) sources
- CTI Reports
- Incident Response historical data
- Analyst infrastructure knowledge
- Indicators tools (forensics, Wireshark, Splunk)

IR Notified based upon Event/Incident Category?

Questions
- Did all searches execute across all available databases?
- Were searches completed in expected timeframe and criticality level?
- Any unexpected "black swan" results?
- What high impact threats were detected/reported?

Data to be captured
- Initial/spot analysis of event
- IT environment(s) impacted
- Escalation to IR and at what categorization
- Search results
    - False positives
    - False Negatives
- All indicators correlated with original IOC data (anomalies noted)

Figure 2. 'Acquire' Workflow and Considerations

Analyze

Once the search has been completed, the CTI analysts will begin the Analyze phase. The fundamental analysis tasks consist of:

- Modify and re-execute searches, if necessary
  - Determine the level of risk to the IT environment
  - Determine the attribution of the attacker by IP addresses, MAC addresses, threat signatures, etc.
  - Validate target matches
  - Correlate contextual intelligence
  - Modify target searches
  - New target activity
  - Sort and "clean" data sets for follow-on data analytics efforts
  - Create updated and new analytic products as needed

- Sort, link, and prioritize data events with threat activities
- Identify additional indicators (IOCs) and target activities
- If necessary, initiate a new hunt based on newly discovered data. *Is the threat based on modified target activity or new specific IOCs?*

The inferential analysis will be performed based on the analyst's knowledge of the environment, operational exposure, and business intelligence factors. Questions that should be asked will include:

- What determination can be made based on facts and empirical data?
- How has the original hunt hypothesis been proven or disproven?
- What key data do we know, and what do we not know?

Predictive Analysis (PA) is the cornerstone of effective analytical work. *If you cannot reasonably predict what the threat will do next, then the developed intelligence provides no value.* The growth of Big Data availability has led to increases in efficiency, effectiveness, and transparency for both the public and private sectors. Predictive Analytics is about technology, mathematics, and models to make better forecasts. It is further about predicting better human behavior that will help companies and agencies make improved and profitable decisions. The challenge is how to make further advances in PA to provide overall enhanced predictive outcomes in decision-making. Also, See Appendix C – "Predictive Analytics: The Potential Role for Process Improvement" for a more extensive discussion of PA.

The remaining tasks during the Analyze phase are to determine infrastructure **attack vectors** and related **Tactics, Techniques, and Procedures (TTPs)** that support future defensive actions to dissuade, deter, and stop the threat. Analysis **correlated** by the CTI analyst may assist in determining threat sources, motivations, and capabilities.

Determine the effectiveness of existing security controls, and if needed, suggest improvements or new security controls. These may include security controls from existing cybersecurity frameworks, including NIST 800-53, NIST 800-171, or ISO 27001. It may be necessary to create new hybrid controls not currently formulated by any existing frameworks. Any new security control should always be aligned and complementary with established security controls.

Metrics: The suggested data fields for compiling metrics are:

- Malicious findings
- Non-malicious findings
- Analytic determinations

- Malware variants identified
- Common IOCs or patterns
- Total IOCs detected
- Vulnerabilities exploited
- Affected/targeted business units
- Intelligence summary data (key points)
- Security control failures and success
- Affected infrastructure
- Affected geographic locations
- Threat actor attribution
- Chronology of exposure

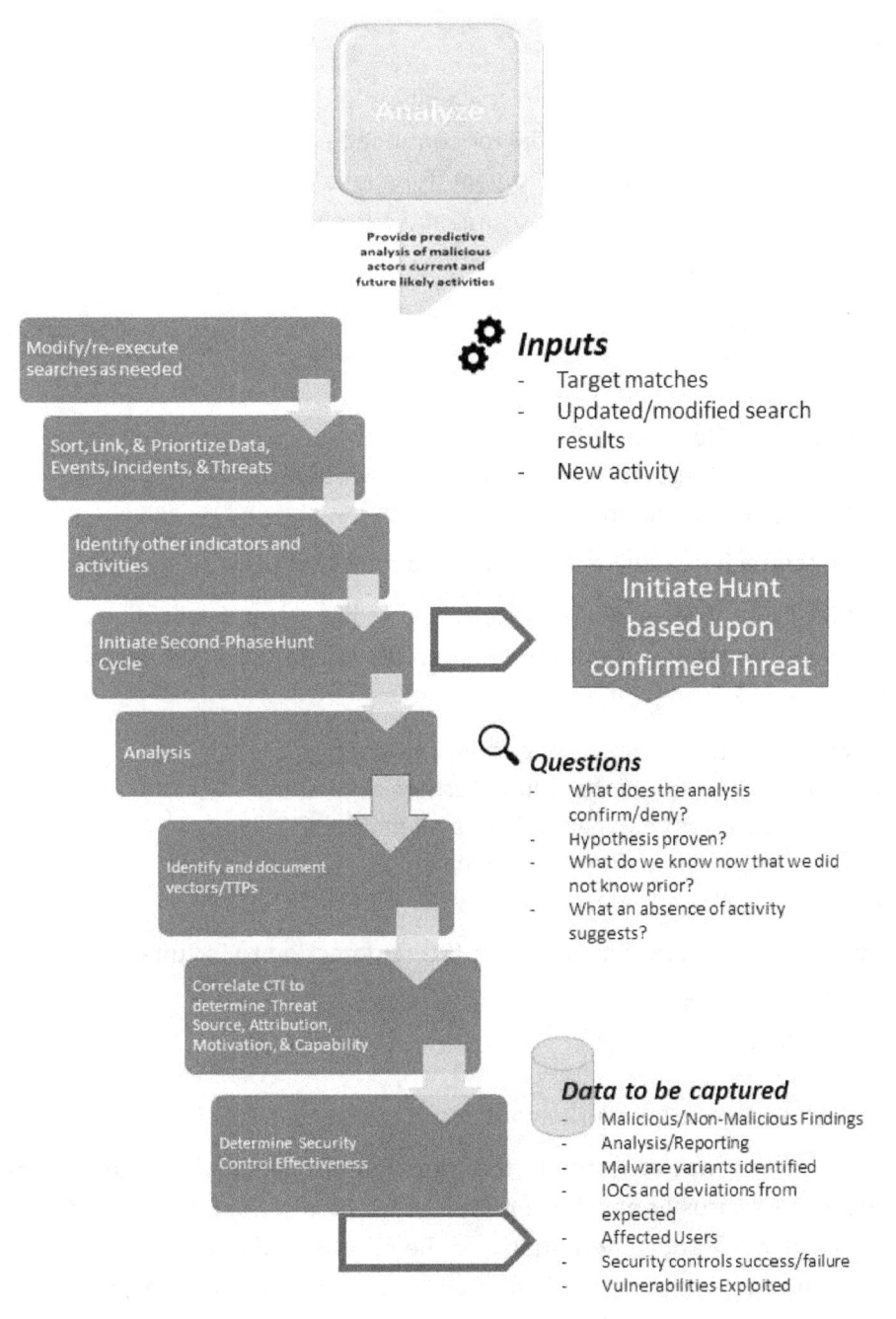

Analyze

Provide predictive analysis of malicious actors current and future likely activities

Modify/re-execute searches as needed

Sort, Link, & Prioritize Data, Events, Incidents, & Threats

Identify other indicators and activities

Initiate Second-Phase Hunt Cycle

Analysis

Identify and document vectors/TTPs

Correlate CTI to determine Threat Source, Attribution, Motivation, & Capability

Determine Security Control Effectiveness

Inputs
- Target matches
- Updated/modified search results
- New activity

Initiate Hunt based upon confirmed Threat

Questions
- What does the analysis confirm/deny?
- Hypothesis proven?
- What do we know now that we did not know prior?
- What an absence of activity suggests?

Data to be captured
- Malicious/Non-Malicious Findings
- Analysis/Reporting
- Malware variants identified
- IOCs and deviations from expected
- Affected Users
- Security controls success/failure
- Vulnerabilities Exploited

Figure 3. 'Analyze' Workflow and Considerations

Reporting

The Reporting phase finalizes the analysis and distributes the reporting. Feedback in this phase is essential for continued process improvement. Determine the overall **business impact** (functional and financial) considering the environment, organizational exposure, and current business intelligence.

Develop a **threat summary**.

- Analytical determinations
- Affected users
- Security control failures/successes
- Geographic locations affected
- Affected or targeted business units or individuals
- Intelligence requirements

Form **strategic outlook** and recommendations based on observed threats.

Identify gaps in strategic (and tactical) intelligence and collections. Formulate new intelligence requirements. General questions that should be asked are:

- What CTI are we missing tactically and strategically?
- What can we automate to limit further exposure?
- How do we communicate this to stakeholders?
- What recommendations do we make?
- Can we improve the process?

Identify data for blocks and alerts for future detection to include:

- CTI portal data
- CTI process elements
- SIEM watch lists
- Blocks or alerts in security controls

The intelligence collected in the hunt can now be analyzed to determine if **new business cases or new base hunts** should be developed. If so, this should be referenced in hunt documentation and the new base hunts/use cases.

The new intelligence should also be used to **update the intelligence lifecycle** with new strategic and tactical CTI. Intelligence is rarely an end-to-end process and operates as a continuous cycle. Updates are part of the constant improvement process necessary to improve all phases of the process.

The analyst next identifies scenarios and indicators to **mitigate future exposure**. While not possible in every case, this topic should be discussed with security engineers, cybersecurity professionals, consultants, and Subject Matter Experts (SME) to explore ways to mitigate future risk to the environment further.

Finally, the CTI analyst will **distribute and deliver intelligence reporting** and gain feedback for process improvement. This will typically result in analytic notes and database updates to the MTHDB. A more extensive incident that has occurred will *require* a formal After-Action Report (AAR) event; AARs are the foundation of practical continual improvement efforts and processes.

Metrics: The following data fields are recommended as candidate metrics for measuring the effectiveness of overall C-THP:

- Realized organizational impact
- Full threat report or threat summary
- Archive of all data collected during the trend analysis
- Report distribution tracking
- New intelligence requirements based on the completed hunt
- After action items (internal and business units)
- Intelligence gaps
- Process or collection gaps
- Stakeholder Requests for Information/Intelligence (RFI) and Product Requests for Changes (RFC)

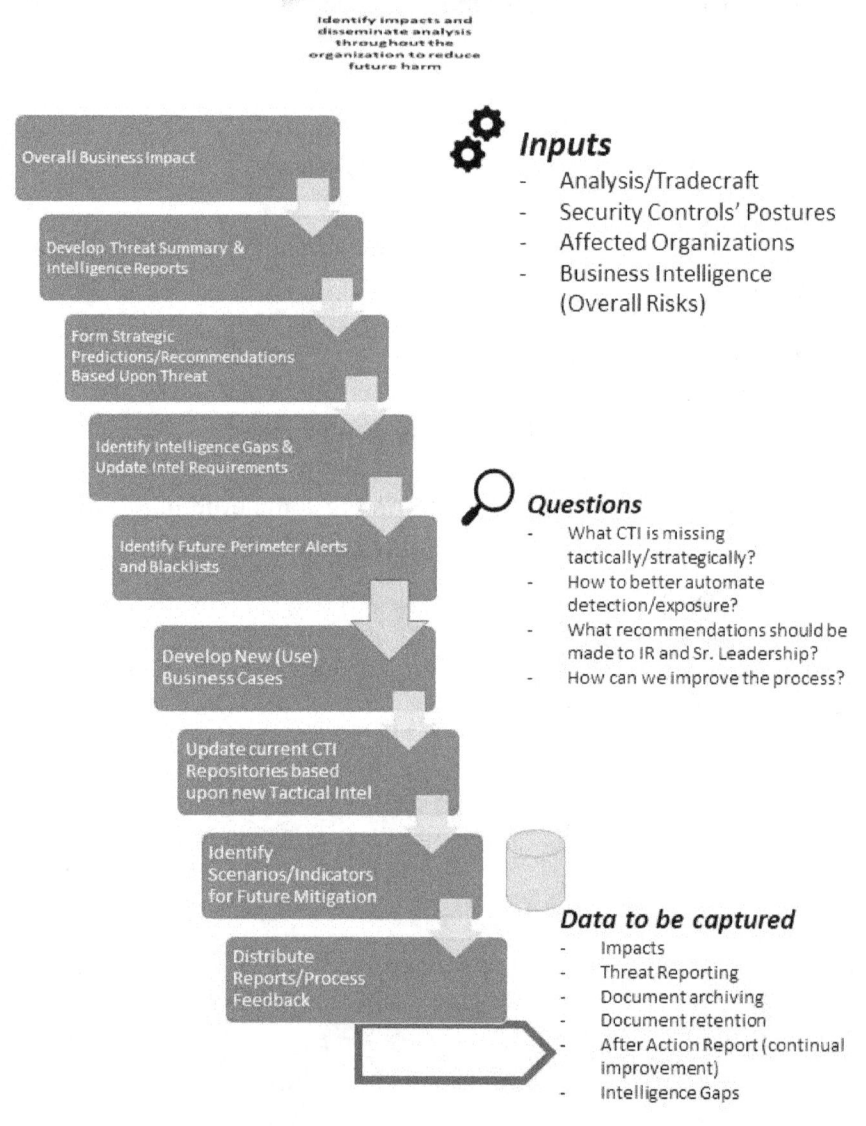

Reporting

Identify impacts and disseminate analysis throughout the organization to reduce future harm

Overall Business Impact

Develop Threat Summary & Intelligence Reports

Form Strategic Predictions/Recommendations Based Upon Threat

Identify Intelligence Gaps & Update Intel Requirements

Identify Future Perimeter Alerts and Blacklists

Develop New (Use) Business Cases

Update current CTI Repositories based upon new Tactical Intel

Identify Scenarios/Indicators for Future Mitigation

Distribute Reports/Process Feedback

Inputs
- Analysis/Tradecraft
- Security Controls' Postures
- Affected Organizations
- Business Intelligence (Overall Risks)

Questions
- What CTI is missing tactically/strategically?
- How to better automate detection/exposure?
- What recommendations should be made to IR and Sr. Leadership?
- How can we improve the process?

Data to be captured
- Impacts
- Threat Reporting
- Document archiving
- Document retention
- After Action Report (continual improvement)
- Intelligence Gaps

Figure 4. **'Reporting' Workflow and Considerations**

PART IV – Mission Planning

The Truly Tactical Portion of C-THP

C-THP Mission Planning

Mission Planning is the foundational aspect of any Threat Hunting activity. It substantiates the effort by documenting all hunts, providing a mechanism to direct and resource the undertaking, and starting-point for the C-THP. The approach offered below is predominantly based upon the United States Army's Military Decision Making Process (MDMP)[23]. The C-THP follows a ten-step process. (See Appendix G for the overall workflow diagram for C-THP Mission Planning).

STEP	Action	Description	Responsible
0	**Collection & Analysis**	Ongoing threat awareness based upon both internal and external data feeds regarding threats to the IT environment. (*This is a continuous and preparatory step*).	CTI
1	**Initiation**	IR authorizes threat hunting activity based upon proactive (base) or reactive responses.	IR (leadership)
2	**Resourcing**	IR identifies allotted commit time, resources, outside SME, etc., to support threat hunt.	IR
3	**Intelligence Analysis**	Review of specific intelligence of likely threats; their means, motives, and opportunities (MMO).	Threat Hunt + CTI
4	**Initial Attribution**	Initial attempt to fix the actual threat and its known capabilities.	Threat Hunt + CTI
5	**Courses of Action (COA)**	Identified COA based upon leadership direction to include	Threat Hunt + CTI (IR final approval)

---

[23] https://en.wikipedia.org/wiki/Military_Decision_Making_Process

		setting boundaries. Should be part of an issued Execution Order (EXORD).	
6	**Planning**	Identify actions on the threat target and the IT environment to meet EXORD objectives.	Threat Hunt + CTI
7	**Execution**	Begin action.	Threat Hunt
8	**Reporting**	Update and create existing or new analytic reports to archive action and support future improvements to C-THP.	CTI
9	**Continual Improvement**	All team members meet to identify ways to improve in the future, documented as part of MHTDB.	Threat Hunt + CTI + IR

The Threat Hunting Mission Planning process provides a conventional means to conduct C-THP operations. It provides an iterative process designed to focus on the three major players of the Threat Hunting effort. It should be used as a powerful means to prepare, conduct, and improve internal hunting activities. It is designed to establish the Threat Hunting Response Engagement & Action Team (THREAT); THREAT is a flexible task organization approach that can be applied based upon available personnel and resourcing constraints.

The "Optimal" THREAT Task Organization

The most common question at this point of any discussion about Threat Hunting is the correct number and types of individuals needed to comprise the overall Threat Hunting team. *The simple answer is the number should be at least 7.* However, it will always *depend* on the agencies, companies, or industries' priorities and resources. **THREAT** is a fully active effort to engage, mitigate, and preferably stop the cyber-threat in the respective IT environment. The task organization will depend on how the core triad of teams, *Incident Response (IR), Cybersecurity Threat Intelligence (CTI),* and

Threat Hunting harmonize their roles. While senior leadership plays the most decisive role, IR is that entry into the Threat Hunting Process.

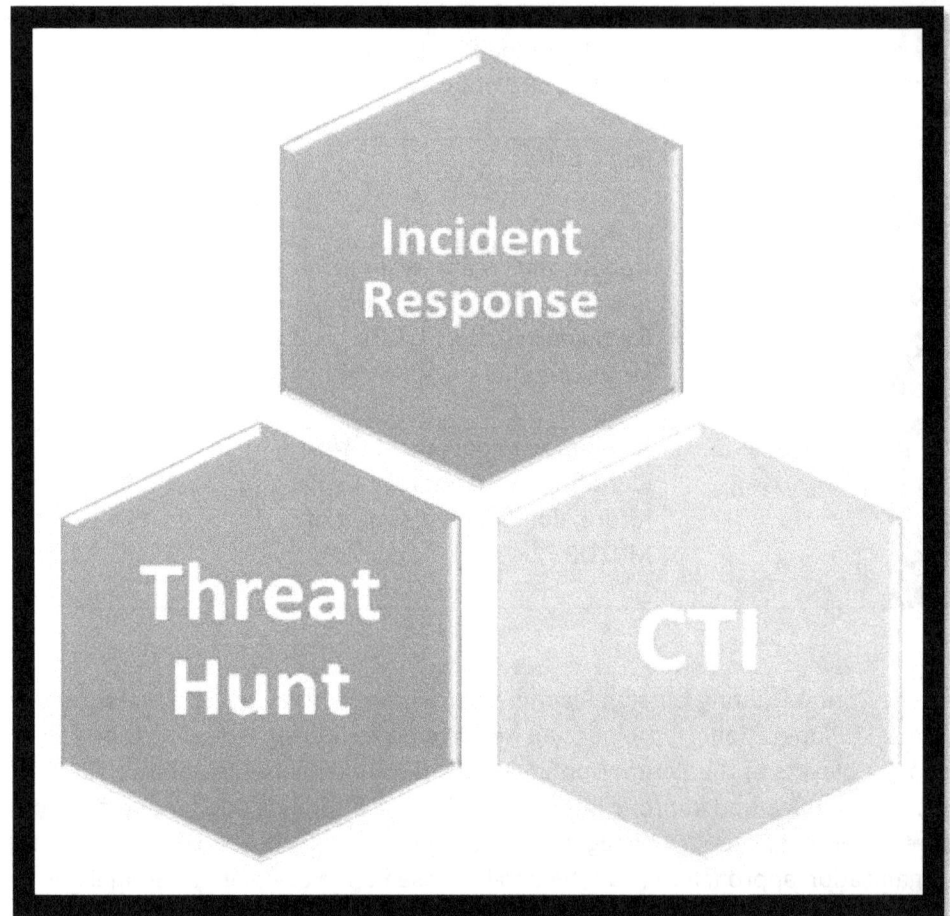

The Three Major Participants in the C-THP

A typical mix of skill sets is outlined and described below. This is designed to be a guide for a company's or agency's leadership.

1. **Team Lead:** This will be designated from within the Threat Hunting organization. This will be a senior leader who understands the rules and responsibilities of the overall Hunt effort. They will ensure that the THREAT effort is conducted per laws, rules, policies, etc., established by the federal and state governments,

agencies, and organizations. They are the first line of defense from improper use of *THREAT* other than meeting a specific Hunt activity's mission objectives.

2. **CTI Lead:** This individual will be the liaison to the primary CTI team. They will review current and past reports to identify anomalies, threat signatures, etc., and provide all pertinent information and intelligence to the team. Once the Hunting is completed, they will be responsible for creating reports to leadership, conducting After Action reporting activities, and updating the MTHDB.

3. **Hunting Technician:** This individual will have elevated system privileges to determine the nature of the cyber-threat. Their skill sets would include access to any Security Information Event Management (SIEM) devices or firewalls for updating policy settings, configurations, etc. This may include, for example, blacklisting or whitelisting actions by both an identified threat and friendly actors. This should consist of applying and using such tools as Nmap, Wireshark, etc., for specific data packet inspection. The Hunting Tech may be supplemented by additional team members based upon the extensiveness of the attack.

4. **Forensics Technician:** This individual would review and monitor all past and current log activities to help both CTI and the Hunting Tech understand the cyber-threats motives and actions better. This information would be used to supplement the CTI effort to identify commonalities and differences between previously identified signature actions of the cyber-threat. This individual would also be responsible for collecting data to be transferred to Law Enforcement (LE), intelligence professionals, etc., based upon any future external actions implemented by the company or agency.

5. **Counterintelligence (CI)/Counter-Cybersecurity Intelligence (CCI) Technician:** This individual would typically be a member of CTI with a deeper understanding of what mechanisms are best to be employed prior, during, and after an attack. They would help better inform the overall THREAT effort of how to best mitigate against like threat cyber-actors. Their role may be combined with CTI based upon resourcing and priorities.

6. **Network Engineer Technician (NET):** This individual should be drawn from the general IT organization with a wide-ranging understanding of the overall network. They would have *root-level* access capabilities and further advise and

support THREAT with advanced programming and scripting knowledge that may be needed during and after a cyber-attack.

7. **Incident Response Liaison (IRL):** The IRL will directly communicate any organizational concerns from senior leadership and ensure compliance with established rules and regulations. The IRL will help avoid any reduction or damage to the THREAT's explicit effort to protect the IT system, network, or environment. They would also coordinate with Human Resources and supervisors where the threat is internal and may require disciplinary or final legal action.

Additionally, the *THREAT* may be supplemented by matrixed personnel from other parts of the organization or, in some cases, SMEs hired to be on-call to support Threat Hunting. Such individuals include:

- Legal
- Law enforcement
- Supervisor (insider threat)
- Third-party (outside) consultant SMEs

The effort of an effectively pre-planned task organization against a cyber-threat is always *optimal* and can never ensure the absolute *best* solution. It will require an agency to ascertain its priorities within its available budgeting for SMEs assigned to the *THREAT*. The objective is to have these specialists identified and have the right expertise to ensure their availability during an assault. This combination of experts would be established to reduce the overall damage to their respective IT environments, ultimately.

PART V – Appendices

Appendix A – Relevant Terms and Glossary

Audit logs   A chronological record of information system activities, including records of system accesses and operations performed in each period.

Authentication   Verifying a user's identity, process, or device is often a prerequisite to allowing access to resources in an information system.

Availability   Ensuring timely and reliable access to and use of information.

Baseline Configuration: A documented set of specifications for an information system, or a configuration item within a system, has been formally reviewed and agreed on at a given point in time, which can be changed only through change control procedures.

Blacklisting   The process used to identify: (i) software programs that are not authorized to execute on an information system; or (ii) prohibited websites.

Confidentiality   Preserving authorized restrictions on information access and disclosure, including protecting personal privacy and proprietary information.

Configuration Management
                            A collection of activities focused on establishing and maintaining the integrity of information technology products and information systems through control of processes for initializing, changing, and monitoring those products and systems' configurations throughout the system development life cycle.

Controlled Unclassified Information (CUI/CDI)

Information that law, regulation, or governmentwide policy requires to have safeguarding or disseminating controls, excluding information classified under Executive Order 13526, Classified National Security Information, December 29, 2009, or any predecessor or successor order, or the Atomic Energy Act of 1954, as amended.

Hardware

The physical components of an information system.

Incident

An occurrence that actually or potentially jeopardizes the confidentiality, integrity, or availability of an information system or the information the system processes, stores, or transmits or constitutes a violation or imminent threat of violation of security policies, security procedures, or acceptable use policies.

Information Security

The protection of information and information systems from unauthorized access, use, disclosure, disruption, modification, or destruction to provide confidentiality, integrity, and availability.

Information System

A discrete set of information resources is organized to collect, process, maintain, use, share, disseminate, or dispense information.

Information Technology
Any equipment or interconnected system or subsystem of equipment used in the automatic acquisition, storage, manipulation, management, movement, control, display, switching, interchange, transmission, or reception of data or information by the executive agency. It includes computers, ancillary equipment, software, firmware, similar procedures, services (including support services), and related resources.

Integrity
Guarding against improper information modification or destruction and includes ensuring information non-repudiation and authenticity.

Internal Network
A network where: (i) the establishment, maintenance, and provisioning of security controls are under the direct supervision of organizational employees or contractors; or (ii) cryptographic encapsulation or similar security technology implemented between organization-controlled endpoints, provides the same effect (at least about confidentiality and integrity).

Malicious Code
Software intended to perform an unauthorized process that will hurt the confidentiality, integrity, or availability of an information system. A virus, worm, Trojan horse, or other code-based entity that infects a host. Spyware and some forms of adware are also examples of malicious code.

Media
Physical devices or writing surfaces include magnetic tapes, optical disks, magnetic disks, and printouts (but not including display media) onto which information is recorded, stored, or printed within an information system.

Mobile Code   Software programs or parts of programs obtained from remote information systems, transmitted across a network, and executed on a local information system without explicit installation or execution by the recipient.

Mobile device   A portable computing device that: (i) has a small form factor such that a single individual can easily carry it; (ii) is designed to operate without a physical connection (e.g., wirelessly transmit or receive information); (iii) possesses local, non-removable or removable data storage; and (iv) includes a self-contained power source. Mobile devices may also have voice communication capabilities, on-board sensors that allow the devices to capture information, or build-in features to synchronize local data with remote locations. Examples include smartphones, tablets, and E-readers.

Nonfederal Information System

An information system that does not meet the criteria for a federal information system. Nonfederal organization.

Network   Information system(s) implemented with a collection of interconnected components. Such components may include routers, hubs, cabling, telecommunications controllers, key distribution centers, and technical control devices.

Privileged Account   An information system account with authorizations of a privileged **user**.

Privileged User   A user authorized (and therefore, trusted) performs security-relevant functions that ordinary users are not authorized to perform. (Also referred to as Elevated Privileges User).

Remote Access   Access to an organizational information system by a user (or a process acting on behalf of a user) communicating through an external network (e.g., the Internet).

Risk   A measure of the extent to which a potential circumstance or event threatens an entity, and typically a function of (i) the adverse impacts that would arise if the circumstance or event occurs; and (ii) the likelihood of occurrence. Information system-related security risks are those risks that arise from the loss of confidentiality, integrity, or availability of information or information systems and reflect the potential adverse impacts to organizational operations (including mission, functions, image, or reputation), corporate assets, individuals, other organizations, and the Nation.

Sanitization   Actions taken to render data written on media unrecoverable by both ordinary and, for some forms of sanitization, extraordinary means. The process of removing information from media such that data recovery is not possible. It includes removing all classified labels, markings, and activity logs.

Security Controls   A safeguard or countermeasure is prescribed for an information system or an organization designed to protect the confidentiality, integrity, and availability of its information and meet a set of defined security requirements.

Security Control Assessment

The testing or evaluation of security controls to determine the extent to which the controls are implemented correctly, operating as intended, and producing the desired outcome concerning meeting the security requirements for an information system or organization.

Security Functions

The hardware, software, or firmware of the information system responsible for enforcing the system security policy and supporting the isolation of code and data on which the protection is based.

Threat

Any circumstance or event with the potential to adversely impact organizational operations (including mission, functions, image, or reputation), organizational assets, individuals, other organizations, or the Nation through an information system via unauthorized access, destruction, disclosure, modification of information, or denial of service.

Whitelisting

The process used to identify: (i) software programs authorized to execute on an information system.

Appendix B – Continuous Monitoring's Importance to the C-THP

Continuous Monitoring (ConMon) is critical to any discussion of Hunting Team activities and operations. ConMon typically provides automated alerts to organizational IT personnel and is intended to provide real-time detection of threat activities. This paper better describes what ConMon is and how it would effectively be deployed in an IT environment. The description here is focused on the Eleven (11) NIST Security Domains and is intended as a primer on mainstream ConMon implementation.

Cybersecurity is not about shortcuts. There are no easy solutions to years of leaders demurring their responsibility to address cyberspace's growing threats. We hoped that the Office of Personnel Management (OPM) breach several years ago would herald the needed focus, energy, and funding to quash the bad-guys. That has proven an empty hope where leaders have abrogated their responsibility to lead in cyberspace. The "holy grail" solution of ConMon has been the most misunderstood solution where too many shortcuts are perpetrated by numerous federal agencies and the private sector to create an illusion of success. This paper is specifically written to help leaders better understand what constitutes a true statement of: "we have continuous monitoring." This is not about shortcuts. This is about education, training, and understanding at the highest leadership levels that cybersecurity is not a technical issue but a leadership issue.

The Committee on National Security Systems defines ConMon as: "[t]he processes implemented to maintain current security status for one or more information systems on which the operational mission of the enterprise depends" (CNSS, 2010). ConMon has been described as the holistic solution of end-to-end cybersecurity coverage and the answer to providing an effective global Risk Management (RM) solution. It promises the elimination of the 3-year recertification cycle that has been the bane of cybersecurity professionals.

For ConMon to become a reality for any agency, it must meet the measures and expectations defined in the National Institute of Standards and Technology (NIST) Special Publication (SP) 800-137, Information Security Continuous Monitoring for Federal Information Systems and Organizations. "Continuous monitoring has evolved as a best practice for managing risk on an ongoing basis" (SANS Institute, 2016); it is an instrument that supports effective, continual, and recurring RM assurances. For any agency to truly espouse it has attained full ConMon compliance, it must coordinate all the described major elements as found in NIST SP 800-137.

ConMon is not just the passive visibility pieces but also includes the active efforts of vulnerability scanning, threat alert, reduction, mitigation, or elimination of a dynamic Information Technology (IT) environment. The Department of Homeland Security (DHS) has couched its approach to ConMon more holistically. Their program to protect government networks is more aptly called: "Continuous Diagnostics and Monitoring" or CDM and includes a need to react to an active network attacker. "The ability to make IT networks, end-points and applications visible; to identify malicious activity; and, to respond [emphasis added] immediately is critical to defending information systems and networks" (Sann, 2016).

Another description of ConMon can be found in NIST's CAESARS Framework Extension: An Enterprise Continuous Monitoring Technical Reference Model (Second Draft). It defines its essential characteristics within the concept of "Continuous Security Monitoring." It is described as a "…risk management approach to Cybersecurity that maintains a picture of an organization's security posture, provides visibility into assets, leverages the use of automated data feeds, monitors the effectiveness of security controls, and enables prioritization of remedies," (NIST, 2012); it must demonstrate visibility, data feeds, measures of effectiveness and allow for solutions. It provides another description of what should be shown to ensure full ConMon designation under the NIST standard.

The government's Federal Risk and Authorization Management Program (Fed-RAMP) has defined similar ConMon goals. These objectives are all key outcomes of a successful ConMon implementation. Its "… goal[s]…[are] to provide: (i) operational visibility; (ii) annual self-attestation on security control implementations; (iii) managed change control; (iv) and attendance to incident response duties," (GSA, 2012). While not explicit to NIST SP 800-37, these objectives are well-aligned with the desires of an effective and complete solution.

RMF creates the structure and documentation needs of ConMon; it represents the specific implementation and oversight of Information Security (IS) within an IT environment. It supports the general activity of RM within an agency. (See Figure 1). The RMF "… describes a disciplined and structured process that integrates information security and risk management activities into the system development life cycle" (NIST-B,

2011). RMF is the structure that both describes and relies upon ConMon as its risk oversight and effective mechanism between IS and RM.

Figure 1. CM "bridges" Information Security and Risk Management

This article provides a conceptual framework to address how an agency would identify a proper ConMon solution through NIST SP 800-137. It discusses the additional need to align component requirements with the *"11 Security Automation Domains"* necessary to implement true ConMon. (See Figure 2). It is through the complete implementation and

Figure 2. The 11 Security Automation Domains (NIST, 2011)

integration with the other described components—See Figure 3 --that an organization can correctly state it has achieved ConMon. incentives

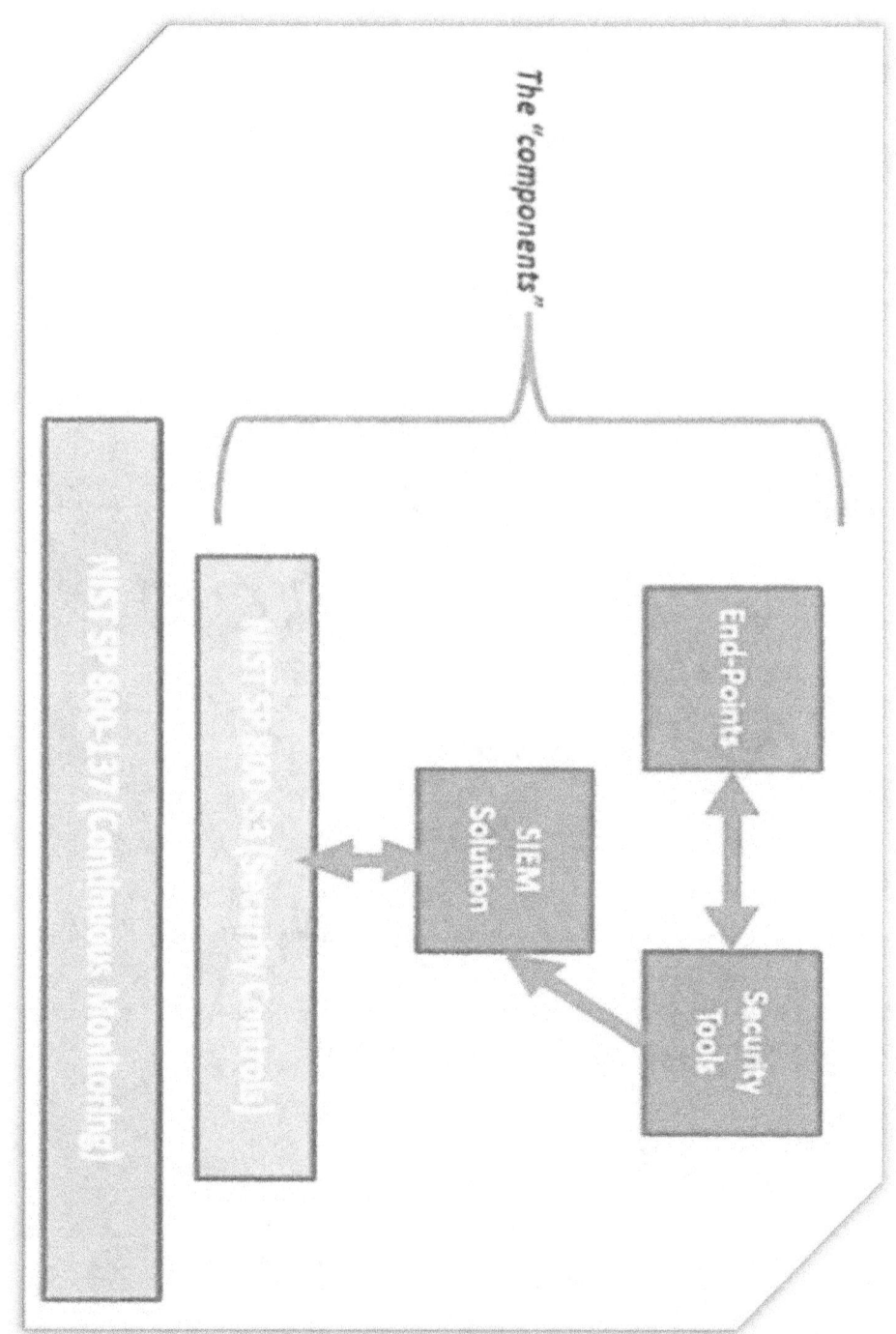

Figure 3. The "Components" of an Effective Continuous Monitoring

For ConMon to be effective and genuine, it must align end-point visibility with security monitoring tools. This includes security monitoring tools with connectivity to "end-points" such as laptops, desktops, servers, routers, firewalls, etc. Additionally, these must work with a highly integrated Security Information and Event Management (SIEM) device. The other "component" is a clear linkage between the end-points, security monitoring tools, and the SIEM appliance, working with the *Security Automation Domains* (See Figure 2). These would include, for example, the areas of malware detection, asset, and event management. ConMon must first address these composite components to create a "First Generation" instantiation.

A SIEM appliance provides the central core data processing capabilities to effectively coordinate all the inputs and outputs from across the IT enterprise. It manages the data integration and interpretation of all ConMon components. And it provides the necessary visibility and intelligence for an operational incident response capability.

End-point devices must be persistently visible to the applicable security devices. Together, these parts must align with the respective security controls described in NIST SP 800-53. The selected SIEM tool must accept these inputs and analyze them against defined security policy settings, recurring vulnerability scans, signature-based threats, and heuristic/activity-based analyses to ensure the environment's security posture. The SIEM outputs must support the IT environment's further visibility, conduct and disseminate vital intelligence, and mindful leadership to any ongoing or imminent dangers. The expression above is designed to provide a conceptual representation of the cybersecurity professional attempting to ascertain effective ConMon implementation or to develop a complete ConMon answer for an agency.

Additionally, the SIEM must distribute data feeds in near-real-time to analysts and key leaders. It provides for multi-level "dashboard" data streams, and issues alert based upon prescribed policy settings. Once these base, First Generation functionalities are consistently aligning with the Security Automation Domains, an organization can definitively express it meets the requirements of ConMon.

End-Points

It is necessary to identify hardware and software configuration items that must be known and constantly traceable before implementing ConMon within an enterprise IT environment. End-point visibility is not the hardware devices but the hardware device's baseline software on the network.

Configuration Management is also a foundational requirement for any organization's security posture. Soundly implemented Configuration Management must be the basis of any complete CM implementation. At the beginning of any IS effort, cyber-professionals must know the current "as-is" hardware and software component state within the enterprise. End-points must be protected and monitored because they are the most valuable target for would-be hackers and cyber-thieves.

Configuration Management provides the baseline that establishes a means to identify potential compromise between the enterprise's end-points and the requisite security tools. "Organizations with a robust and effective [Configuration Management] process need to consider information security implications concerning the development and operation of information systems including hardware, software, applications, and documentation" (NIST-A, 2011).

The RMF requires the categorization of systems and data as high, moderate, or low regarding risk. The Federal Information Processing Standards (FIPS) Publication 199 methodology is typically used to establish the federal government's data sensitivity levels. FIPS 199 aids the cybersecurity professional in determining data protection standards of both end-points and the data stored in these respective parts. For example, a system that collects and retains sensitive data, such as financial information, requires a higher security level. End-points must be recognized as repositories of highly valued data to cyber-threats.

Further, cyber-security professionals must be constantly aware of the "...administrative and technological costs of offering a high degree of protection for all federal systems..." (Ross, Katzke, & Toth, 2005). This is not a matter of recognizing the physical end-point alone but the value and associated costs of the virtual data stored, monitored, and protected continually. FIPS 199 helps system owners determine whether a higher level of protection is warranted, with higher associated costs, based upon an overall FIPS 199 evaluation.

Security Tools

Security monitoring tools must identify in near-real-time an active threat. Examples include anti-virus or anti-malware applications used to monitor network and end-point activities. Products like McAfee and Symantec provide enterprise capabilities that help to identify and reduce threats.

Other security tools would address in whole or part the remaining NIST Security Automation Domains. These would include, for example, tools to provide asset visibility, vulnerability detection, patch management updates, etc. But it is also critical to recognize that even the best current security tools are not necessarily capable of defending against all attacks. New malware or zero-day attacks pose continual challenges to the cybersecurity workforce.

For example, DHS's EINSTEIN system would not have stopped the 2015 Office of Personnel Management breach. Even DHS's latest iteration of EINSTEIN, EINSTEIN 3, an advanced network monitoring and response system designed to protect federal governments' networks, would not have stopped that attack. "...EINSTEIN 3 would not have been able to catch a threat that [had] no known footprints, according to multiple industry experts" (Sternstein, 2015).

Not until there are a much greater integration and availability of cross-cutting intelligence and more capable security tools can any single security tool ever be fully effective. The need for multiple security monitoring tools that provide "defense in depth" may be a better protective strategy. However, with various tools monitoring the same Security Automation Domains, such an approach will undoubtedly increase the costs of maintaining a secure agency or C/U IT environment. A determination of Return on Investment (ROI) balanced against a well-defined threat risk scoring approach is further needed at all federal and C/U IT workspace levels.

Security Controls

"Organizations are required to adequately mitigate the risk arising from the use of information and information systems in the execution of missions and C/U functions" (NIST, 2013). This is accomplished by selecting and implementing NIST SP 800-53, Revision 4, described security controls. (See Figure 4). They are organized into eighteen families to address sub-set security areas such as access control, physical security, incident response, etc. The use of these controls is typically tailored to the respective system owner's security categorization relying upon FIPS 199 categorization standards. A higher security categorization requires the greater implementation of these controls.

ID	FAMILY	ID	FAMILY
AC	Access Control	MP	Media Protection
AT	Awareness and Training	PE	Physical and Environmental Protection
AU	Audit and Accountability	PL	Planning
CA	Security Assessment and Authorization	PS	Personnel Security
CM	Configuration Management	RA	Risk Assessment
CP	Contingency Planning	SA	System and Services Acquisition
IA	Identification and Authentication	SC	System and Communications Protection
IR	Incident Response	SI	System and Information Integrity
MA	Maintenance	PM	Program Management

Figure 4. Security Control Identifiers and Family Names (NIST, 2013)

Security Information and Event Management (SIEM) Solutions

The SIEM tool plays a pivotal role in any viable "First Generation" implementation. Based on NIST and DHS guidance, a capable SIEM appliance must provide the following functionalities:

- "Aggregate data from "across a diverse set" of security tool sources;
- Analyze the multi-source data;
- Engage in explorations of data based on changing needs
- Make quantitative use of data for security (not just reporting) purposes, including the development and use of risk scores; and
- Maintain actionable awareness of the changing security situation on a real-time basis" (Levinson, 2011).

"Effectiveness is further enhanced when the output is formatted to provide information that is specific, measurable, actionable, relevant, and timely" (NIST, 2011). The SIEM device is the vital core of a total solution that collects, analyzes, and alerts the cyber-professional of potential and actual dangers in their environment.

Several major SIEM solutions can effectively meet the requirements of NIST SP 800-137. They include products, for example, IBM® Security, Splunk®, and Hewlett Packard's® ArcSight® products.

For example, Logrhythm ® was highly rated in the 2014 SIEM evaluation. Logrhythm® provided network event monitoring and alerts of potential security compromises. Implementing an enterprise-grade SIEM solution is necessary to meet growing cybersecurity requirements for auditing security logs and capabilities to respond to cyber-incidents. SIEM products will continue to play a critical and evolving role in the demands for "...increased security and rapid response to events throughout the network" (McAfee® Foundstone Professional Services®, 2013). Improvements and upgrades of SIEM tools are critical to providing a more highly responsive capability for future generations of these appliances in the marketplace.

Next Generations

Future generations of ConMon would include specific expanded capabilities and functionalities of the SIEM device. These second generation and beyond evolutions would be more effective solutions in future dynamic and hostile network environments. Such advancements might also include increased access to a greater pool of threat database signature repositories or more expansive heuristics to identify functional anomalies within a target network.

Another futuristic capability might include the use of Artificial Intelligence (AI). Improved SIEM capabilities with AI augmentation would further enhance human threat analysis and provide for more automated responsiveness. "The concept of predictive analysis involves using statistical methods and decision tools that analyze current and historical data to make predictions about future events…" (SANS Institute). The next generation would boost human response times and abilities to defend against attacks in a matter of milli-seconds vice hours.

Finally, in describing the next generations of ConMon, it is not only imperative to expand data, informational, and intelligence inputs for new and more capable SIEM products, but that input and corresponding data sets must also be thoroughly vetted for completeness and accuracy. Increased access to signature and heuristic activity-based analysis databases would provide a more significant risk reduction. More substantial support from the private industry and the Intelligence Community would also be significant improvements for Agencies that are continually struggling against a more-capable and better-resourced threat.

ConMon will not be a reality until vendors and agencies can integrate the right people, processes, and technologies. "Security needs to be positioned as an enabler of the organization—it must take its place alongside human resources, financial resources, sound C/U processes and strategies, information technology, and intellectual capital as the elements of success for accomplishing the mission" (Caralli, 2004). ConMon is not just a technical solution. It requires capable organizations with trained personnel, creating effective policies and procedures with the requisite technologies to stay ahead of cyberspace's growing threats.

Figure 6 provides a graphic depiction of what ConMon components are needed to create a holistic NIST SP 800-137-compliant solution; this demonstrates the First-Generation representation. Numerous vendors describe that they have the "holy grail" solution. Still, until they can prove they meet this description in total, they are unlikely to complete a comprehensive ConMon solution yet.

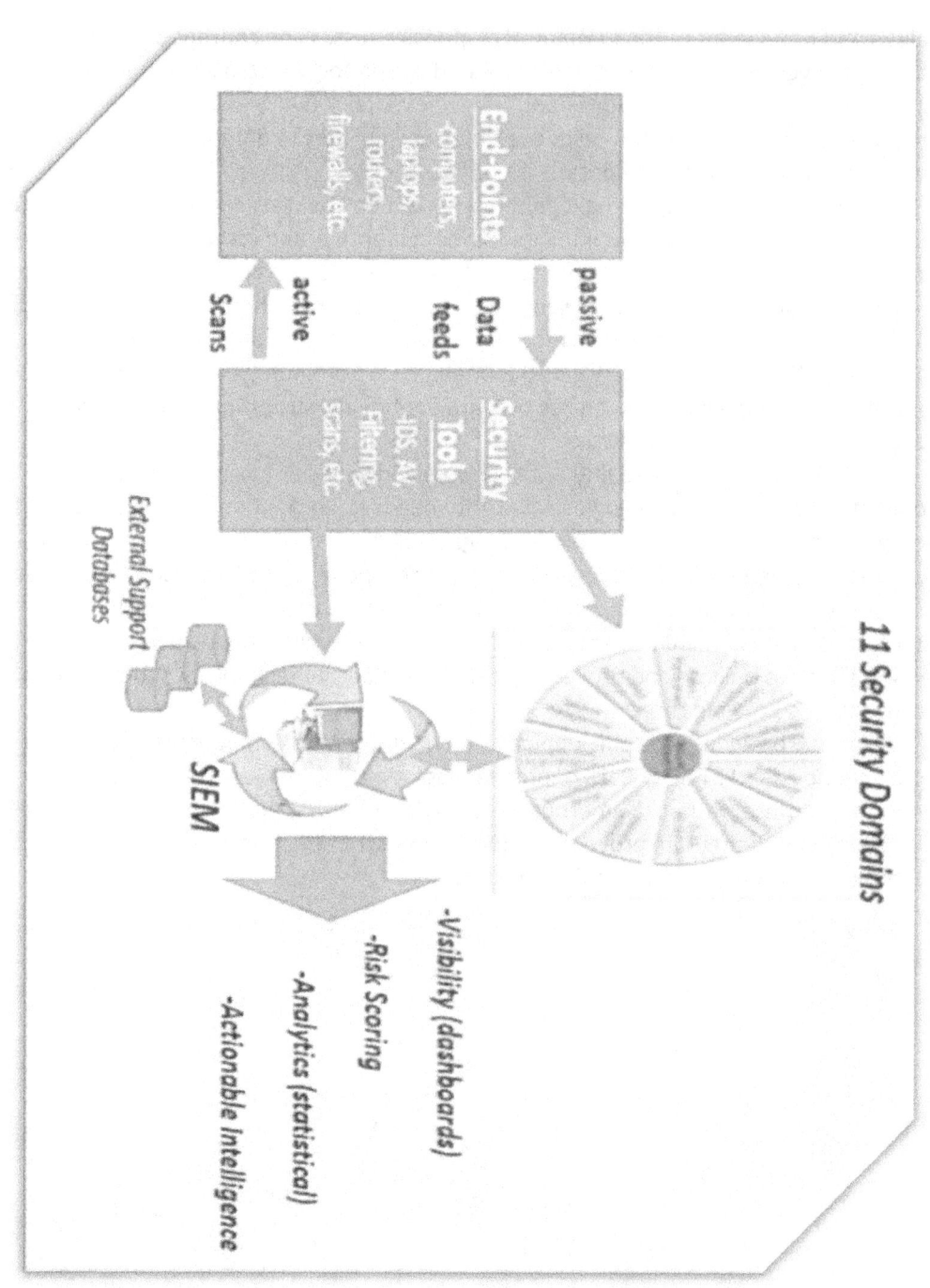

First Generation Continuous Monitoring

References for "Continuous Monitoring and the C-THP"

Balakrishnan, B. (2015, October 6). *Insider Threat Mitigation Guidance*. Retrieved from SANS Institute Infosec Reading Room: https://www.sans.org/reading-room/whitepapers/monitoring/insider-threat-mitigation-guidance-36307

Caralli, R. A. (2004, December). *Managing Enterprise Security (CMU/SEI-2004-TN-046)*. Retrieved from Software Engineering Institute: http://www.sei.cmu.edu/reports/04tn046.pdf

Committee on National Security Systems. (2010, April 26). *National Information Assurance (IA) Glossary.* Retrieved from National Counterintelligence & Security Center: http://www.ncsc.gov/nittf/docs/CNSSI-4009_National_Information_Assurance.pdf

Department of Defense. (2014, March 12). *DOD Instructions 8510.01: Risk Management Framework (RMF) for DoD Information Technology (IT).* Retrieved from Defense Technical Information Center (DTIC): http://www.dtic.mil/whs/directives/corres/pdf/851001_2014.pdf

GSA. (2012, January 27). *Continuous Monitoring Strategy & Guide, v1.1.* Retrieved from General Services Administration: http://www.gsa.gov/graphics/staffoffices/Continuous_Monitoring_Strategy_Guide_072712.pdf

Joint Medical Logistics Functional Development Center. (2015). JMLFDC Continuous Monitoring Strategy Plan and Procedure. Ft Detrick, MD.

Kavanagh, K. M., Nicolett, M., & Rochford, O. (2014, June 25). *Magic Quadrant for Security Information and Event Management.* Retrieved from Gartner: http://www.gartner.com/technology/reprints.do?id=1-1W8AO4W&ct=140627&st=sb&mkt_tok=3RkMMJWWfF9wsRolsqrJcO%2FhmjTEU5z17u8lWa%2B0gYkz2EFye%2BLIHETpodcMTcVkNb%2FYDBceEJhqyQJxPr3FKdANz8JpRhnqAA%3D%3D

Kolenko, M. M. (2016, February 18). *SPECIAL-The Human Element of Cybersecurity*. Retrieved from Homeland Security Today.US: http://www.hstoday.us/briefings/industry-news/single-article/special-the-human-element-of-cybersecurity/54008efd46e93863f54db0f7352dde2c.html

Levinson, B. (2011, October). *Federal Cybersecurity Best Practices Study: Information Security Continuous Monitoring.* Retrieved from Center for Regulatory Effectiveness: http://www.thecre.com/fisma/wp-content/uploads/2011/10/Federal-Cybersecurity-Best-Practice.ISCM_2.pdf

McAfee® Foundstone® Professional Services. (2013). *McAfee.* Retrieved from White Paper: Creating and Maintaining a SOC: http://www.mcafee.com/us/resources/white-papers/foundstone/wp-creating-maintaining-soc.pdf

NIST. (2011-A, August). *NIST SP 800-128: Guide for Security-Focused Configuration Management of Information Systems.* Retrieved from NIST Computer Security Resource Center: http://csrc.nist.gov/publications/nistpubs/800-128/sp800-128.pdf

NIST. (2011-B, September). *Special Publication 800-137: Information Security Continuous Monitoring (ISCM) for Federal Information Systems and Organizations.* Retrieved from NIST Computer Security Resource Center: http://csrc.nist.gov/publications/nistpubs/800-137/SP800-137-Final.pdf

NIST. (2012, January). *NIST Interagency Report 7756: CAESARS Framework Extension: An Enterprise Continuous Monitoring Technical Reference Model (Second Draft).* Retrieved from NIST Computer Resource Security Center: http://csrc.nist.gov/publications/drafts/nistir-7756/Draft-NISTIR-7756_second-public-draft.pdf

NIST. (2013, April). *NIST SP 800-53, Rev 4: Security and Privacy Controls for Federal Information Systems.* Retrieved from NIST: http://nvlpubs.nist.gov/nistpubs/SpecialPublications/NIST.SP.800-53r4.pdf

Ross, R., Katzke, S., & Toth, P. (2005, October 17). *The New FISMA Standards and Guidelines Changing the Dynamic of Information Security for the Federal Government.* Retrieved from Information Technology Promotion Agency of Japan: https://www.ipa.go.jp/files/000015362.pdf

Sann, W. (2016, January 8). *The Key Missing Piece of Your Cyber Strategy? Visibility.* Retrieved from Nextgov: http://www.nextgov.com/technology-news/tech-insider/2016/01/key-missing-element-your-cyber-strategy-visibility/124974/

SANS Institute. (2016, March 6). *Beyond Continuous Monitoring: Threat Modeling for Real-time Response.* Retrieved from SANS Institute: http://www.sans.org/reading-room/whitepapers/analyst/continuous-monitoring-threat-modeling-real-time-response-35185

Sternstein, A. (2015, January 6). *OPM Hackers Skirted Cutting-Edge Intrusion Detection System, Official Says.* Retrieved from Nextgov: http://www.nextgov.com/cybersecurity/2015/06/opm-hackers-skirted-cutting-edge-interior-intrusion-detection-official-says/114649/

Appendix C -- Predictive Analytics: The Potential Role for Process Improvement

Big Data availability has led to increases in efficiency, effectiveness, and transparency for both the public and private sectors (Lee, 2015). Predictive Analytics (PA) is about technology, mathematics, and models to make better forecasts. It is further about predicting better human behavior that will help companies make improved and profitable decisions (Siegel, 2013). The challenge is how to make further advances in PA to provide overall enhanced predictive outcomes in decision-making.

Arithmetic has been worked for centuries within the understandings and improvements of mathematics and statistics to aid man's ability to use the available data. With the vast expansion of the data, we can now infer and better predict outcomes due to the Big Data "revolution." Further, this has supported improvements in the models and algorithms that have provided an ability to measure humans' inherent uncertainty and variability; this is the "technology" component.

Since the beginning of time, man has been enamored with the desire to foretell the future with oracles, wise men, and spiritual leaders that had a supposed connection with the divine. However, it was not until the early 20th Century that the "people" component was recognized as a contributor to improving PA's secular and rational improvements. In 1906, Sir Francis Galton conducted an experiment where several hundred individuals attempted to determine the final weight of a slaughtered cow. The result was greater accuracy from the collective crowd. With remarkable precision, the average weight guessed by the participants was 1,197 pounds, and in fact, the actual weight was 1,198 pounds (Tetlock & Gardner, 2016). This type of "crowd-sourcing" effect demonstrated the informed and knowledgeable average of all people-based predictions that successfully culminated into a final and near-accurate answer.

The only factor that has yet to be fully introduced is the component of an improved process. The solution to a significant evolution in PA may be hiding "in plain sight." While the process is presumed part of the two prior components, the final part may be found in the process that binds these two together. The classic People-Process-Technology (PPT) Triad may always have been in front of us, but we may have just missed this next dimension to improving the ability to make better forecasts; sometimes, the most straightforward answer may be the correct answer or at least the following best path to pursue.

The People-Process-Technology Triad

The PPT Triad has a less than defined origin (Bravo, 2013); however, it has proven valuable in creating holistic solutions to other modern-day problems. In cybersecurity, for example, it is used as a methodology to solve incomplete security controls. It provides a means to address controls where a technological solution may not eliminate or mitigate a finding, such as a lack of *two-factor authentication*. For example, the leadership can leverage better training for its employees about password protection (people) and company policies that provide stern punishment if an employee does not regularly change their passwords (process). The PPT Triad forms the basis of this paper's approach to the next phased improvement to the area of PA. See Figure 1 (Russo, 2014).

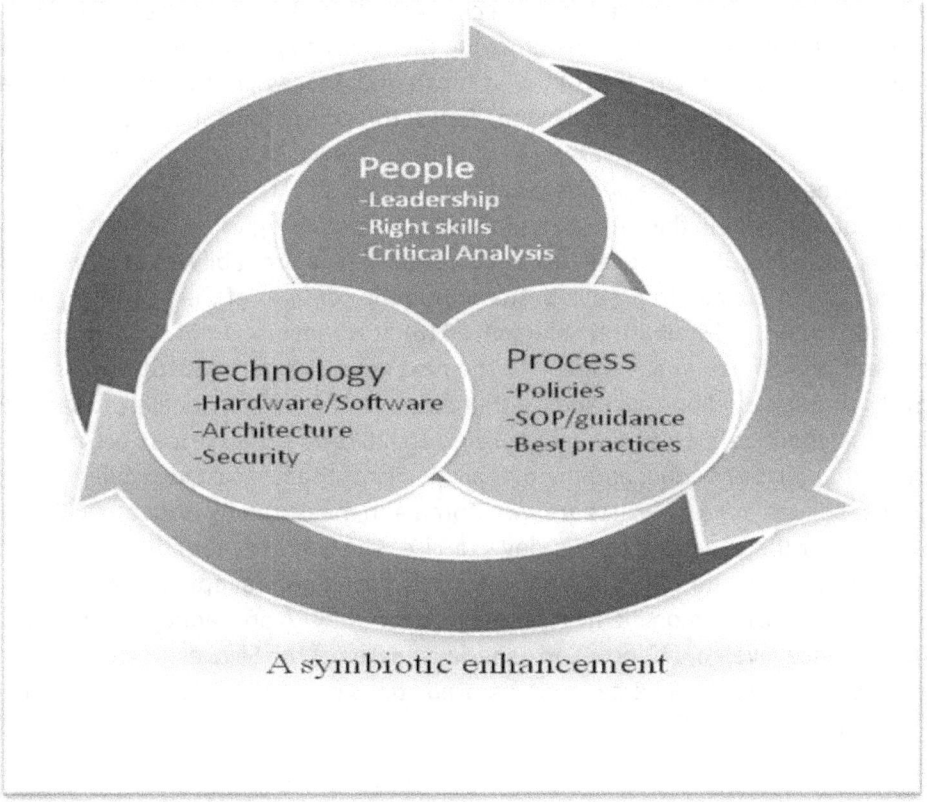

Figure 1. The PPT triad. Reprinted from "Cloud Computing Should Not Be Used to Address Weaknesses in People and Processes within the Intelligence Community (IC)" by M.A. Russo, p. 4. Copyright 2014 by M.A. Russo.

While Halladay (2013) ignores process improvement, Lee (2015) emphasizes a "systematic approach [that] needs to be taken for projects [and solutions]..." (p. 13). He implies the process of solving the problem of an improved approach to better predictions. The answer for improved PA may be found within the process component to include, for example, better policies, guidance, and best practices that have yet to be a significant focus of the data analytics community.

Brief History

The enhancements in mathematics' can be seen in the current growth and demand for Artificial Intelligence (AI), data science, and data analytics as an outcome of the Big Data collection, analysis, and reporting revolution. However, all of this has not just been a technological occurrence, but a change in how these fields perceive and better accept the human element in improving the ability to predict the future. It was not until the work of Hubbard (2016) that a substantial process improvement occurred due to his training approach of "calibrated" SMEs; this *process* enhancement in predictive forecasting is a simple example of the occurrence of how the *process* can become concealed behind the *people* component of the PPT Triad.

Hubbard's work in this area is significant. While he recognizes that most individuals, including SMEs, are initially bad at determining probabilities to a future event, they can be trained to predict better within the confines of the possibility and their unique expertise (Hubbard & Seiersen, 2016). It is reminiscent of Sir Galton's earlier described efforts, and it is taken to the next level. Hubbard (2016) and his team take SMEs through a calibration exercise that refines both the individual's probabilistic predictive skills and refines it (Hubbard & Seiersen, 2016). As the exercise progresses, more information is provided, and the overall quality of the forecast improves.

These progressive forecasts are monitored and measured by Hubbard's (2016) team even after the initial one to two-day exercise. The SMEs are found to improve based upon these scientifically and psychologically developed calibration exercises. As Hubbard discussed, common elements that interfere with PA are reduced to include underconfidence, overconfidence, and especially biases of the SME estimators that would have an otherwise adverse effect on predictions (Hubbard & Seiersen, 2016).

The Three Branches

There are three distinct branches defined in the field of business analytics. They are **descriptive**, **predictive**, and **prescriptive** (Praseeda & Shivakumar, 2014); this is where *predictive analysis* exists. This paper concentrates on the predictive but recognizes the vital importance of the others. Descriptive addresses the past and the data of a same or similar occurrence that can contribute to PA's prediction portion. The predictive focus on the "what if," or the unknowns to be answered by either the statistical mathematics, the SME forecasts, or both (Praseeda & Shivakumar, 2014). The prescriptive help determine the follow-on actions to solve or reduce a problem or issue's negative impacts. Without the prior or the latter of PA, this process flow would not provide any real or actionable insights to the business or organization.

PA relies upon the "priors" of the descriptive data collected by the data scientist. Any advanced "...learning process is initiated by incorporating past [information and] errors in the evaluation of incoming or new data and changes..." (Lee, 2015, p. 16). The prescriptive is the pathway that occurs due to the outputs of PA. Without the past, applied to the present, the future desire for actionable results would be meaningless and useless.

It Must Be Actionable

PA is about creating actionable information that the business can benefit from (Halladay, 2013; Praseeda & Shivakumar, 2014). Halladay (2013) describes that business intelligence relies upon PA to provide a holistic view of the company to make better decisions. Process improvement must move PA's state to a next and better point that enhances the current decision-making demands of businesses or organizations.

Halladay's (2013) research focused on equipment leasing and the finance industry. Specifically, PA's objective is to support corporate leadership to make better future commercial decisions about risk and profitability. His work only calls out the technology and people components. However, it does highlight the lack of detailed research in process improvement to enhance PA and suggests a new area requiring more academic and applied research.

In Plain Sight

The answer to improving the ability to make better predictions has been within our grasp, but we have failed to recognize it because it may have just appeared too obvious. The PPT Triad suggests that a solution to a problem may be found by applying a technological, people, or process solution either individually or in combination. The process component's challenge is that it is already part of the statistical mathematics used today in PA. It would include, for example, the processes such as the transitive, substitution, and reflexive properties of mathematics that are already procedures embedded in the very nature of the applied mathematics and statistics. This may be why we have not explored this path more directly. Process improvement should refine the predictive ability of data scientists, statisticians, and corporate leadership, and we did not notice it as a next step.

But even if this lost variable holds the solution, it is essential to be mindful of the absolute dangers. We can never be categorically 100% able to predict a highly variant and fluid future. Before exploring potential process improvements, there is a need to understand "process outcome paradoxes" (Tetlock & Gardner, 2016). Tetlock and Gardner (2016) describe in their book, *Superforecasting*, that "[n]othing is one hundred percent" (p. 134). Both the current state of technology and people components of the PPT Triad already recognize this by measuring probability and the inclusion of uncertainty (Hubbard & Seiersen, 2016). Forecasts can get better but can never reach "God-like" predictive capabilities no matter how good the three components of the Triad are improved upon or progress.

Process Improvements

An initial qualitative improvement should begin with the leadership's understanding, execution, and accountability for implementing an active PA effort. One year after the 2015 Office of Personnel Management (OPM) data breach, the then-Acting Director Beth Cobert stated that: "[t]here's a whole series of things around technology, around people, and process that are different today than a year ago" (Naylor, 2016). While Ms. Cobert recognized the importance of the PPT Triad to address this significant data breach, the information already existed that should have stopped or at least vastly reduced the effectiveness of this critical historical cybersecurity breach. This included the best practice implementation of two-factor authentication, an already well-known best practice by the government. *Did it require a significant exfiltration of millions of personnel data records to cause this?*

The first process improvement should begin with leaders' accountability to provide the needed support and recognition of the PA effort. Halladay (2013) describes that corporate leadership must both include PA into the decision-making process and further accept those outputs without "second-guessing or ignoring the predictive analytics" (p. 5). Before the process can improve, the strategic understanding and employment should be ingrained as part of the business or organizational culture.

Secondarily, Bayesian mathematics relies on the "priors." Past information is applied primarily in Bayesian mathematics to help the technology and the people component improve the prediction quality. This is *not* an unrealistic best practice and is based upon logic. As newer and verified information is provided to the predictive model, it will improve the output's quality and fidelity.

The same can be described for SMEs. They retain a large body of knowledge as experts as they learn and grow within their respective study areas. SMEs can and will refine their predictions as Lee discusses that PA is an "iterative process" that combines sampling, estimation, and predictiveness into a single cohesive model (Lee, 2015). His conceptual model for a Predictive Analytics System (PAS) affords the best example of creating a refined process that can ensure PA efforts' repeatability (p. 13).

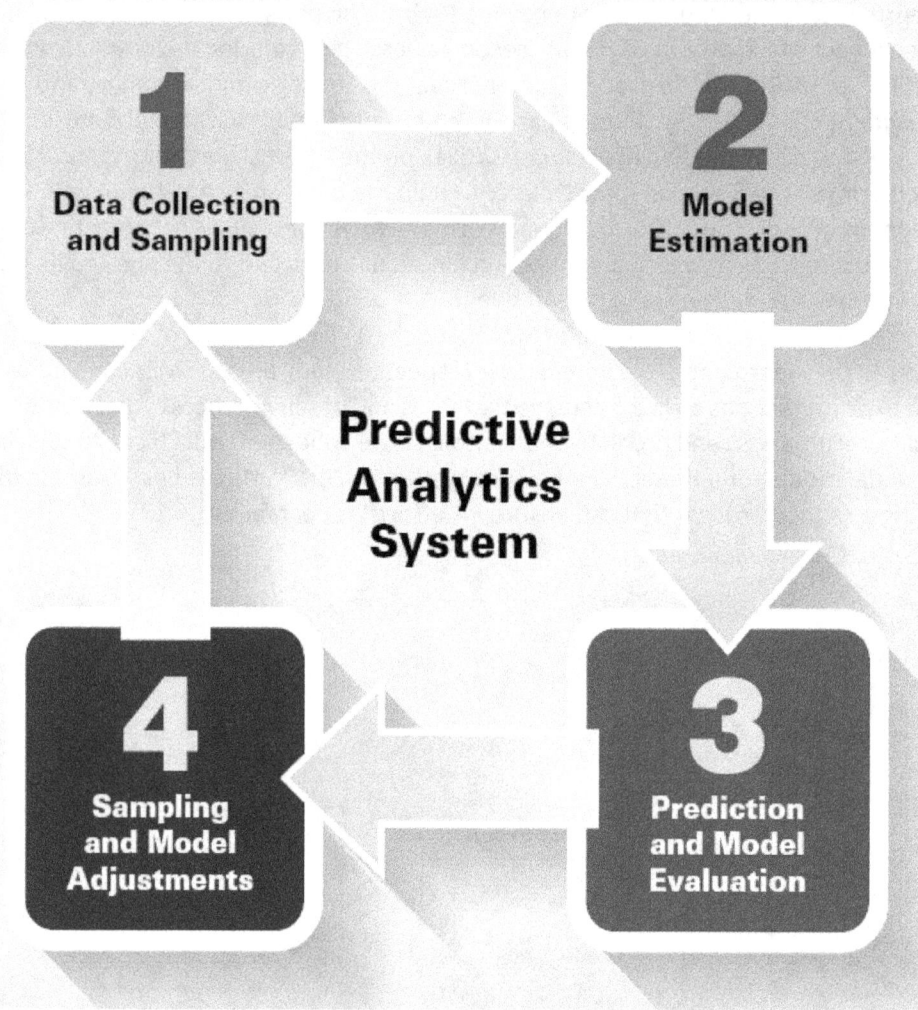

Figure 2. Predictive analytics system. Reprinted from "Predictive analytics: The new tool to combat fraud, waste, and abuse," by A.J. Lee, 2015, *Journal of Government Financial Management,* Summer Edition, p. 13. Copyright 2015 by the Association of Government Accountants.

    A final recommended process improvement may appear necessary for a data scientist. Still, as noted in the 2015 OPM breach, while it was already recognized that two-factor authentication was required, OPM (and much of the US government) had not implemented it. The suggested removal of predictions outside the norm, not their elimination from consideration, should occur. The common term is "outlier." Any forecast, either mathematical or SME-based, that appears outside of the general estimate should be set aside because such an outlook would most likely skew the overall prediction.

However, we need to be reminded that outlier estimates should be removed to improve the process, *but* it must also be recognized that these outliers sometimes come true. Examples such as the 1941 surprise attack on Pearl Harbor or the September 11, 2001 attack would have been an extreme outlier or "black swan" event (Taleb, 2007). Outliers should be considered but *typically* should not be part of any final prediction.

Conclusion

PA will improve if the processes between the technology and the people are better melded. While the earlier two pillars of the PPT Triad have afforded significant improvements in humans' predictive capabilities, the next step may be found in the *internal* and *external* processes that can provide that next significant evolutionary advance. Improved processes and sub-processes, i.e., policies, best practices, procedures, etc., are the likely next phase of enhanced PA development.

It may seem an obvious answer, but the works of Hubbard and Seiersen (2016) and Tetlock and Gardner (2016) recognize the connection needed between the two earlier PPT components. The next phase of advances in the process is the most likely evolutionary step required to improve PA's value for better decision-making; this would be both of a quantitative nature, improving the mathematics, and qualitative nature, improving upon the SME. The SME, cybersecurity expert, data scientist, or corporate officer will be able to get near to them but never reach a "perfect" prediction. However, they will have an improved overall mechanism through this next progression in determining better predictions to support the future needs of corporate and organizational decision-making.

References for "Predictive Analytics: The Potential Role of Process Improvement"

Bravo, M. A. (2013, September 8). *Who created the People - Process - Technology framework?* Retrieved from Quora: https://www.quora.com/Who-created-the-People-Process-Technology-framework

Halladay, S. D. (2013). Using predictive analytics to improve decision-making. *The Journal of Equipment Lease Financing (Online)*, 31(2), B1-B6. Retrieved from https://search.proquest.com/docview/1413251757?accountid=44888

Hubbard, D., & Seiersen, R. (2016). *How to measure anything in cybersecurity risk.* Hoboken, NJ: John Wiley & sons.

Lee, A. J. (2015). Predictive analytics: The new tool to combat fraud, waste and abuse. *The Journal of Government Financial Management*, 64(2), 12-16. Retrieved from https://search.proquest.com/docview/1711620017?accountid=44888

Naylor, B. (2016, June 6). *One year after OPM data breach, what has the government learned?* Retrieved from National Public Radio: https://www.npr.org/sections/alltechconsidered/2016/06/06/480968999/one-year-after-opm-data-breach-what-has-the-government-learned

Praseeda, C., & Shivakumar, B. (2014). A review of trends and technologies in business analytics. *International Journal of Advanced Research in Computer Science*, 5(8). Retrieved from https://search.proquest.com/docview/1658426584?accountid=44888

Russo, M. A. (2014). *Cloud computing should not be used to address weaknesses in people and processes within the intelligence community (ic).* (Unpublished master's program submission). Retrieved from self. Washington, DC.

Siegel, E. (2013). *Predictive analytics: The power to predict who will click, buy, lie, or die.* Hoboken: Wiley.

Silver, N. (2012). *The signal and the noise: Why so many predictions fail--but some don't.* New York: Penguin.

Taleb, N. N. (2007). *The black swan: The impact of the highly improbable (Vol. 2).* New York: Random house.

Tetlock, P., & Gardner, D. (2016). *Superforecasting: The art and science of prediction.* New York: Random house.

Appendix D -- Can the Human "Poet" Bring Value to Predictive Analysis?

From the time we are children through adulthood, we are reminded that that which cannot be measured cannot be managed appropriately. (This is the core of why metrics must be a vital part of C-THP). The United States Congress, for example, repeatedly calls for better measurements and metrics; however, they do not appear to subsequently predict or at least foresee the next financial crisis, a political coup, or cybersecurity attack with these numbers alone. It is not just the absence of such data but the lack of employment of the human element's qualitative strengths.

The predictive forecasting and modeling community recognize the value that humans bring to the field of data analytics. As Hubbard and Seiersen (2016) state: "...if the primary concern about using probabilistic methods is the lack of data, then you also lack the data to use non-quantitative methods" (p. 38). The "human element" is the derived and non-quantitative component that is needed.

There are several reasons the often biased, irrational, and poetic human will continue to contribute to the quantitative quality. This includes the individual subject matter expert's value, the collective synergy of a larger sample of experts, and man's innate innovativeness in attempting to solve problems and reject the status quo. Humans do not detract from the calculations but provide their unique recognition and context to both the inputs and the results.

Hubbard & Seiersen (2016) and Tetlock & Gardner (2016) identify the importance of the "calibrated" subject matter expert to improve the state of predictive analysis. Such an individual is proficient in their field and has been trained to understand a significant facet of quantitative measurement: uncertainty. These individuals are described by Tetlock (2016) as the "superforecasters." Silver (2012) recognizes that forecasting is not about absolute mathematical precision. Still, the acknowledgment of the importance of knowing that "[w]e must become more comfortable with probability **and** [emphasis added] uncertainty" (p. 15); the individual understands the role of uncertainty where the mathematical equation or model does not. This uncertainty helps others understand the super forecaster's expected deviation, specifically, as the norm and not the exception to actual accuracy.

It is also the collective nature of human beings attempting to solve problems that continue to contribute to better predictive analytic outcomes. In 1906, the British Scientist, Sir Francis Galton, conducted an experiment where he had several hundred individuals attempt to determine a slaughtered cow's final weight. The result was greater accuracy from the collective crowd. With remarkable precision, the average weight guessed by the participants was 1197 pounds, and in fact, the actual weight was 1198 pounds (Tetlock & Gardner, 2016). This type of "crowd-sourcing" effect demonstrates the informed and knowledgeable average of all guesses (or predictions) culminated into a final and near-accurate answer. This collective "hive mind" shows how the accumulation of human knowledge can be brought together to enhance the precision of the result directly.

Additionally, Christakis and Fowler (2009) recognize that individual humans are an essential component of quantified and predictive outcomes, but even greater results are possible jointly. "...[C]hallenges require us to recognize that although human beings are individually powerful, we must act together to achieve what we could not accomplish on our own" (p. 304). The more experts contributing to a predictive analytical formula or algorithm will more likely add to greater accuracy less any identified uncertainty.

In the book, *Moneyball* (Lewis, 2004), Billy Beane, the coach of the Oakland A's baseball team, successfully employed the rigors of data analysis and statistics to propel his team to its historical twenty games winning streak where it was one of the worst-ranked teams at the time (Thum, 2012). The challenges were many, but he knew that following the old models of human instinct, hunches, and guesswork in selecting the best players was not going to solve his biggest problem—not having the larger payrolls that other big-league teams had to recruit the "best" players (Lewis, 2004).

Beane also identified that baseball scouting "...was at roughly the same stage of development in the twenty-first century as professional medicine was in the eighteenth" (Lewis, 2004, p. 17). His recruiting of Paul DePodesta, a Harvard graduate with a love of math, statistics, and baseball, was a recognition that there was a need for innovation. This innovation riled his internal scouting staff (Lewis, 2004). His ultimate and revolutionary acknowledgment of DePodesta's mathematical approaches was so effective for the improvement of the Oakland A's successful winning on the playing field.

The human element in the CTI analyst (CTI analyst) form will always be a vital part of data analytical and predictive improvements. With the exponential growth and access to data and the fledgling data science community's power, it will bring needed value to the development of such analyses. Future predictive analytic progress will rely upon the unique abilities man presents, and it will directly result in better forecasts. These better forecasts will be a consequence of man's ability to grow and improve his world's real state around him.

References for "Can the Human Poet Bring Value to Predictive Analysis?"

Christakis, N., & Fowler, J. (2009). *Connected; The surprising power of our social networks and how they shape our lives.* New York: Little, Brown & Company.

Hubbard, D., & Seiersen, R. (2016). *How to measure anything in cybersecurity risk.* Hoboken, NJ: John Wiley & sons.

Lewis, M. (2004). *Moneyball: The art of winning an unfair game.* New York: WW Norton & Company.

Silver, N. (2012). *The signal and the noise: Why so many predictions fail--but some don't.* New York: Penguin.

Tetlock, P., & Gardner, D. (2016). *Superforecasting: The art and science of prediction.* New York: Random House.

Thum, W. (2012, August 19). *Ten years later: The A's 20-game winning streak, Scott Hatteberg, and Moneyball.* Retrieved from SBNATION.com: https://www.sbnation.com/2012/8/19/3250200/ten-year-anniversary-athletics-20-game-winning-streak-hatteberg-moneyball

Appendix E – The Threat Hunting Execution Order Template

SENSITIVITY/SECURITY MARKINGS

Copy ___ of ___ Copies

Date:_____

Organization:_____

THREAT HUNTING EXECUTION ORDER (#000001-2020-A)

References: *(These should be added to document all Threat Hunting aspects; some items may be referred to based upon SOP and established architectural and artifact documents).*

- **Network Topology Diagram: (See Annex A)**
- **Privileged User Password List (See Annex B)**
- **Contact Numbers (See Annex C)**
- **Cyber Deception Plan (See Annex D)**
- **Threat Assessment Report (See Annex E [See Appendix F])**
- **Issued Warning Orders (if given)**

Time Zone Used (□ **Z**(GMT)):_____

1. **TYPE HUNT:** □ **HUNT** (EXTERNAL THREAT) □ **BASE HUNT** (INTERNAL)
   □ **BASE HUNT** (AD HOC/RECON) □ **HUNT** (EXERCISE)

2. □ **IMMEDIATE TASK:** □ *DEFEAT (STOP)* □ Confirm attribution
   □ Divert (Cyber-Deception Plan [CDP]) □ Quarantine □ Dissuade □ Disrupt

3. **ALLOCATED TIME:** _____

    a. EXTENSION AUTHORIZED: _____

    b. AUTHORITY: _____

    c. NOTES: _____

4. **SITUATION:**

    a. THREAT

        i. LIKELY THREAT:

        _____

            1. IP Addresses: _____

            2. MAC Addresses: _____

            3. Other attributable data: _____

            _____

        ii. POTENTIAL THREATS:

        _____

        iii. THREAT HISTORY: ☐ **NEW** ☐ **EXISTING** ☐ **UNKNOWN**

            1. _____

            _____

            _____

        iv. LIKELY OBJECTIVES: ☐ **FINANCIAL** ☐ **DATA** ☐ **DESTRUCTION**

           ☐ **EXFIL** ☐ **MODIFICATION** ☐ **ELEV. PRIV.** ☐ **EST. FOOTHOLD**

           ☐ **ATK REPUTATION** ☐ **DOS/DDOS** ☐ **UNKNOWN**

           OTHER: _____

v.　MAJOR APPROACHES:

　　　　　_____

　　　　　_____

　　　　　_____

　　　vi.　Threat Assessment Report (TAR) – (See Appendix E)

　b.　ASSIGNED HUNTING TEAM

　　　i.　Threat Hunting Members (Required):

　　　　　1.　Team Lead:

　　　　　　　_____

　　　　　2.　CTI Lead:

　　　　　　　_____

　　　　　3.　Hunting Technician(s):

　　　　　　　_____

　　　　　4.　Forensics Tech(s):

　　　　　　　_____

　　　　　5.　Counterintelligence (CI)/Counter-Cybersecurity
　　　　　　　Intelligence (CCI) Tech:

　　　　　　　_____

　　　　　6.　Network Engineer Technician (NET):

　　　　　　　_____

　　　　　7.　Incident Response Liaison (IRL):

　　　　　　　_____

    ii. Threat Hunting Support Element (Optional):

        1. Legal:

        _____

        2. Law Enforcement:

        _____

        3. Supervisor (Insider Threat):

        _____

        4. SME/Consultant:

        _____

    iii. Threat Hunting On-Call:

        1. XXX:

        _____

        2. XXX:

        _____

5. MISSION STATEMENT: *(The mission statement should explain the who, what, where, when, and why of the threat hunting action is required, and its major [singular] objective)*

☐ **DEFEAT** ☐ Confirm attribution ☐ Divert ☐ Quarantine ☐ Dissuade ☐ Deter ☐ Disrupt

_____
_____
_____
_____
_____

6. COORDINATION: *(Coordination with federal, state, law enforcement entities based upon established policies and laws, as required/applicable).*
   a. Agency
   b. Law Enforcement
   c. Others

7. SENIOR LEADERSHIP: (Designated leaders authorized to make any calls regarding Threat Hunting activities, potential liabilities, resourcing, time extensions, etc.)

8. APPROVAL: (The most senior leader designated at Threat Hunting Authorization Official (THAO).

REVIEWED BY:	APPROVED BY:
NAME:	NAME:
POSITION:	POSITION:
DATE:	DATE:
CONTACT:	CONTACT:
SIGNATURE:	SIGNATURE:

- **ANNEX A – Network Topology Diagram**
- **ANNEX B – Privileged User Password List (RESTRICTED)**
- **ANNEX C – Contact Numbers**
- **ANNEX D – Cyber Deception Plan**
- **ANNEX E – Threat Assessment Report (TAR)**
- **ANNEX F – Warning Orders Issued**

Appendix F – Threat Assessment Report (TAR)

1. **Likely attribution**: (actual threat to include its ability to spoof its identity. Its physical and virtual locations, locations if known. Data that connects threat to available information to have connections with IOC.)

2. **Possible attribution:** (Other likely threats that this "target" may be based upon forensic analyses of files, scripting languages used, embedded foreign languages, or other digital fingerprinting data provided.)

3. **Strategic capabilities**: (To conduct effective operations against the IT infrastructures).

4. **Best Courses of Action:** (What are the best actions to execute based upon historical, intelligence, or other high-confidence sources? See the spectrum below as a general reference).

   i. Passive
   ii. Defensive
   iii. Active
   iv. Active-Passive Defensive
   v. Active Defensive
   vi. Passive-Defensive

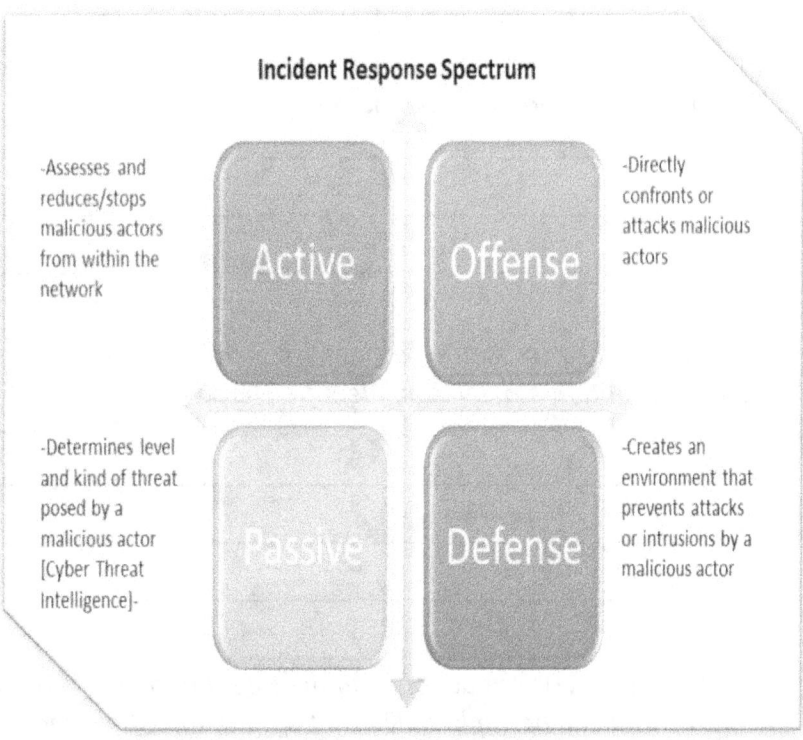

Incident Response Spectrum

-Assesses and reduces/stops malicious actors from within the network

Active

Offense

-Directly confronts or attacks malicious actors

-Determines level and kind of threat posed by a malicious actor [Cyber Threat Intelligence]-

Passive

Defense

-Creates an environment that prevents attacks or intrusions by a malicious actor

(REMOVE WHEN FINAL)

5. Disposition, Composition, and Strength

(a) **Disposition**: *(What you currently know about how the enemy is laid out on the ground and what it says about his general intent and capability. State in most significant detail known to you and down to a level important to your subordinates (at least one level down; two down, if practical)*

_____

_____

_____

(b) **Composition**: *(What organic, supporting, and reinforcing assets are available to the threat? Other hackers?)*

_____

_____

_____

(c) **Strengths:** *(technical capabilities; obfuscation from attribution; resources; nation-state vice unidentified hacker(s)).*

_____

_____

_____

6. **Capabilities**: *(What actions can the threat execute? What weaknesses exist that can be exploited? What are the threat's vulnerabilities?)*

_____

_____

_____

7. **Most Probable Courses of Action**: *(Includes those actions that the threat will likely take in sequence to include essential reactions to Threat Hunting activities).*

_____

_____

_____

_____

_____

_____

_____

_____

_____

_____

_____

8. **Most Dangerous Course of Action**: (*Those actions that the threat can reasonably accomplish but is not likely to execute. This would more appropriately answer your agency or company's question of: "What would cause you to depart significantly from your current hunt actions?" What additional portions of the Incident Response Plan would need to be activated and other resources needed (contingences)?"*).

_____

_____

_____

_____

_____

_____

_____

Appendix G – The 10-Step Threat Hunting Mission Planning Workflow

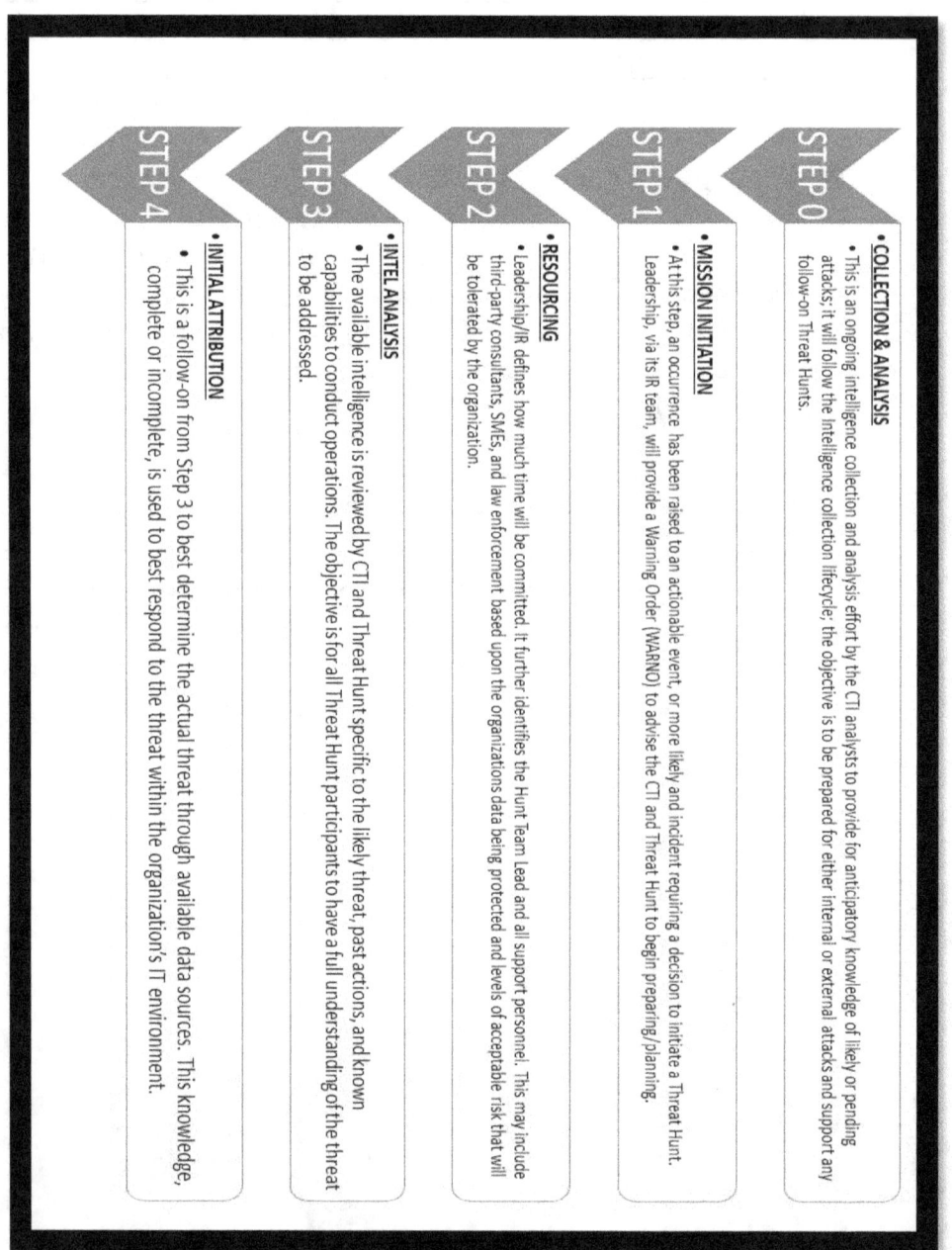

STEP 0

- **COLLECTION & ANALYSIS**
- This is an ongoing intelligence collection and analysis effort by the CTI analysts to provide for anticipatory knowledge of likely or pending attacks; it will follow the Intelligence collection lifecycle; the objective is to be prepared for either internal or external attacks and support any follow-on Threat Hunts.

STEP 1

- **MISSION INITIATION**
- At this step, an occurrence has been raised to an actionable event, or more likely and incident requiring a decision to initiate a Threat Hunt. Leadership, via its IR team, will provide a Warning Order (WARNO) to advise the CTI and Threat Hunt to begin preparing/planning.

STEP 2

- **RESOURCING**
- Leadership/IR defines how much time will be committed. It further identifies the Hunt Team Lead and all support personnel. This may include third-party consultants, SMEs, and law enforcement based upon the organizations data being protected and levels of acceptable risk that will be tolerated by the organization.

STEP 3

- **INTEL ANALYSIS**
- The available intelligence is reviewed by CTI and Threat Hunt specific to the likely threat, past actions, and known capabilities to conduct operations. The objective is for all Threat Hunt participants to have a full understanding of the threat to be addressed.

STEP 4

- **INITIAL ATTRIBUTION**
- This is a follow-on from Step 3 to best determine the actual threat through available data sources. This knowledge, complete or incomplete, is used to best respond to the threat within the organization's IT environment.

Steps 0-4 of Threat Hunting Mission Planning

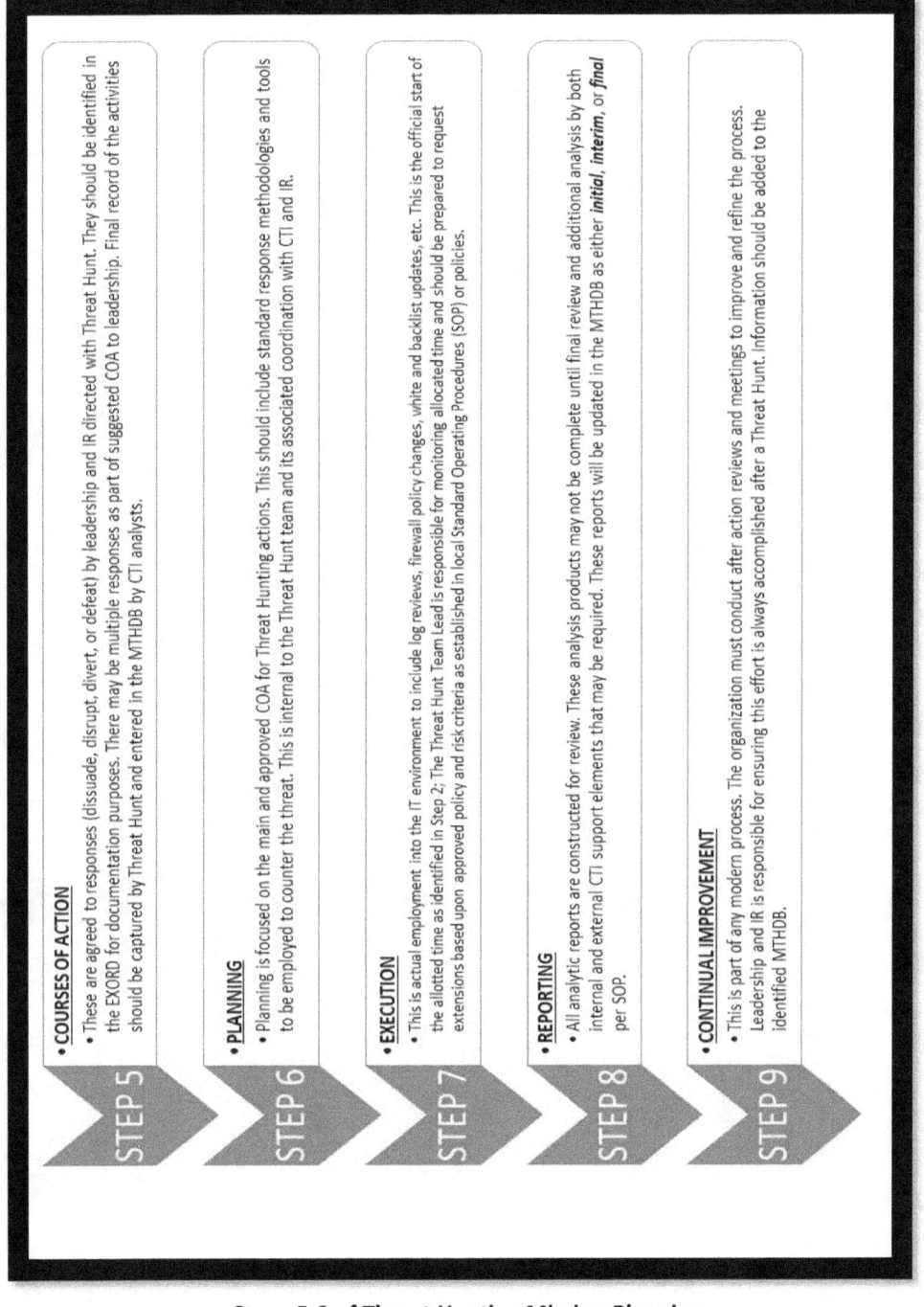

STEP 5 — COURSES OF ACTION
- These are agreed to responses (dissuade, disrupt, divert, or defeat) by leadership and IR directed with Threat Hunt. They should be identified in the EXORD for documentation purposes. There may be multiple responses as part of suggested COA to leadership. Final record of the activities should be captured by Threat Hunt and entered in the MTHDB by CTI analysts.

STEP 6 — PLANNING
- Planning is focused on the main and approved COA for Threat Hunting actions. This should include standard response methodologies and tools to be employed to counter the threat. This is internal to the Threat Hunt team and its associated coordination with CTI and IR.

STEP 7 — EXECUTION
- This is actual employment into the IT environment to include log reviews, firewall policy changes, white and backlist updates, etc. This is the official start of the allotted time as identified in Step 2; The Threat Hunt Team Lead is responsible for monitoring allocated time and should be prepared to request extensions based upon approved policy and risk criteria as established in local Standard Operating Procedures (SOP) or policies.

STEP 8 — REPORTING
- All analytic reports are constructed for review. These analysis products may not be complete until final review and additional analysis by both internal and external CTI support elements that may be required. These reports will be updated in the MTHDB as either *initial*, *interim*, or *final* per SOP.

STEP 9 — CONTINUAL IMPROVEMENT
- This is part of any modern process. The organization must conduct after action reviews and meetings to improve and refine the process. Leadership and IR is responsible for ensuring this effort is always accomplished after a Threat Hunt. Information should be added to the identified MTHDB.

Steps 5-9 of Threat Hunting Mission Planning

About the Author

Mr. Russo is a Chief Data Scientist supporting the DOD with advanced data analytics and technical expertise to identify Tactics, Techniques, and Procedures posed by global cyber-threats. He is a former Senior Information Security Engineer within the Department of Defense's (DOD) F-35 Joint Strike Fighter program. He has an extensive background in cybersecurity and is an expert in the Risk Management Framework (RMF) and DOD Instruction 8510, which implements RMF throughout the DOD and the federal government. He holds both a Certified Information Systems Security Professional (CISSP) certification and a CISSP in information security architecture (ISSAP). He has a 2017 certificate as a Chief Information Security Officer (CISO) from the National Defense University, Washington, DC. He retired from the US Army in 2012 as a Senior Intelligence Officer.

He is the former CISO at the Department of Education, wherein 2016; he led the effort to close over 95% of the outstanding US Congressional and Inspector General cybersecurity shortfall weaknesses spanning as far back as five years.

In 2011, Mr. Russo was certified by the Office of Personnel Management as a graduate of the Senior Executive Service Candidate program.

Mr. Russo was the first-ever Program Executive Officer (PEO)/Senior Program Manager in the Office of Intelligence & Analysis at Headquarters, Department of Homeland Security (DHS), Washington, DC. Mr. Russo was responsible for the development and deployment of secure Information and Intelligence support systems for OI&A to include software applications and systems to enhance the DHS mission. He was responsible for the program management development lifecycle during his tenure at DHS.

He holds a Master of Science from the National Defense University in Government Information Leadership with a concentration in Cybersecurity and a Bachelor of Arts in Political Science with a minor in Russian Studies from Lehigh University. He holds Level III Defense Acquisition certification in Program Management, Information Technology, and Systems Engineering. He has been a member of the DOD Acquisition Corps since 2001.

System Security Plan (SSP) Template & Workbook NIST-based

"SSP" is designed to provide more specific direction and guidance on completing the core NIST 800-171 artifact, the System Security Plan (SSP). This is part of an ongoing series of support documents being developed to address the recent changes and requirements levied by the Federal Government on contractors wishing to do business with the government. These supplements intend to provide immediate and valuable information, so business owners and their Information Technology (IT) staff need. The changes are coming rapidly for cybersecurity contract requirements. Are you ready? We plan to be ahead of the curve with you with high-quality books that can provide immediate support to the ever-growing challenges of cyber-threats to the Government and your business.

The Agile/Security Development Life Cycle (A/SDLC): Integrating Security Functionality into the SDLC ~SECOND EDITION (2019)

In this SECOND EDITION of THE AGILE SECURITY DEVELOPMENT LIFE CYCLE (A/SDLC), we expand and include new information to improve the concept of "Agile Cyber." We further discuss the need for a Security Traceability Requirements Matrix (SecRTM) and the need to know where all data elements are located throughout your IT environment to include Cloud storage and repository locations. The author continues his focus upon ongoing shortfalls and failures of "Secure System Development." The author seeks to use his over 25 years in the public and private sector program management and cybersecurity to create a solution. This book provides the first-ever integrated operational-security process to enhance the reader's understanding of why systems are poorly secured. Why have we, as a nation, missed the mark in cybersecurity? Why nation-states and hackers are successful daily? This book also describes the two dominant mainstream "agile" NIST frameworks that can be employed and how to use them effectively under a Risk Management approach. We may be losing "battles, " but maybe it's time we genuinely commit to winning the cyber-war.

www.ingramcontent.com/pod-product-compliance
Lightning Source LLC
Chambersburg PA
CBHW081000170526
45158CB00010B/2851